The Tzniyus Book

Also by Rabbi Jack Abramowitz

The Nach Yomi Companion
Vol. 1: Neviim—Prophets
Vol. 2: Kesuvim—Writings

The Tzniyus Book

Rabbi Jack Abramowitz

Copyright © 2009 by Rabbi Jack Abramowitz.

ISBN: Softcover   978-1-4415-7796-2

All rights reserved. No part of this book may be reproduced or transmitted in any form or by any means, electronic or mechanical, including photocopying, recording, or by any information storage and retrieval system, without permission in writing from the copyright owner.

This book was printed in the United States of America.

To order additional copies of this book, contact:
Xlibris Corporation
1-888-795-4274
www.Xlibris.com
Orders@Xlibris.com
54260

Contents

Foreword 9

Author's Preface 11

About the Language in this Book 13

The Torah Does Too Say So! 15

What is This Tzniyus, Anyway? 19
    Selected Torah Sources on Tzniyus 23
    Selected Torah Sources on the Power of the Human Body 26
    Selected Torah Sources on the Power of Clothing 30

The Difference 37
    Selected Torah Sources on Men and Women 43

Community Standards 45
    Selected Torah Sources on Community Standards 50

Who Wears the Pants in Your Family? 51
    Selected Torah Sources pertaining to Women Wearing Pants 57

Sing, Sing a Song 59
    Selected Torah Sources Regarding Kol Isha 65

In the Shul: SheLo Asani Isha and Mechitza 67
    Selected Torah Sources on Separating the Genders 72

The Myth of "Shomer Negiah" 73
    Selected Torah Sources pertaining to Kiruv Basar ("Negiah") and Other Sexual Issues 80

A Chapter for the Boys 85

Appendix A: Additional Sources on Tzniyus 91
Appendix B: Role Models from Tanach 97
Appendix C: Immodesty 101

Foreword

by Rabbi Dr. Tzvi Hersh Weinreb
Executive Director Emeritus, Orthodox Union

Leave it to Rabbi Jack Abramowitz to accomplish the nearly impossible. The task involves a set of standards. Consider a topic which many these days think is old-fashioned, even archaic. Add to it the intimate nature of the issue, its long history, and its technical complexity. Then add the challenge of making its discussion readable, comprehensible, and enjoyable, even to a teenage audience. Surely a very difficult task. Yet our author, "Rabbi Jack," as he is known to his colleagues at the Orthodox Union, has pulled it off.

One of the central components of traditional Jewish behavior is personal modesty. Indeed, the prophets considered "walking modestly with God" a *sine qua non* of religiously desirable behavior. One aspect of modesty concerns conduct in the area of interaction with members of the opposite gender. The *halachic* tradition has applied the concept of modesty to dress, language, posture, and even gait. The observant Jew must be careful in his or her self-presentation to society in every aspect of his or her lifestyle.

Resistance to these standards, and the perception of them as unduly harsh and restrictive, is understandable and has long historical roots. Particularly in our postmodern age, when old standards are seen as relativistic and unnecessarily inhibiting, we are witness to a reluctance to abiding by the standards of personal modesty laid out by the *halacha*.

There is thus currently a twofold need.

Firstly, an explication in clear and candid terms of what is acceptable and what is forbidden in the social relationships between men and women.

This explication must be based upon impeccably authoritative sources. It would not be wise to interpret these sources in an overly strict manner, nor would it be honest to render an excessively lenient reading.

Secondly, a treatment of this issue must be persuasive. The reader must be convinced that conforming to the standards, in spite of the fact that they all are so different from familiar norms, is the right thing to do. Adolescents especially, sensitive as they are to fitting in with their peers, must not only be convinced, but inspired to adopt a lifestyle which will potentially result in the disdain and mockery of friends.

Rabbi Abramowitz, who has a remarkable track record of producing excellent introductory materials on a wide range of Jewish topics, has managed to write a book which fulfills both needs. It is based upon a wide variety of sources, going back to the Bible and Talmud and continuing to include contemporary religious authorities. Amazingly, his book is eminently readable and spiritually uplifting.

We at the Orthodox Union are proud of the literary and educational contributions that the author has made to the library of materials for those who seek an authentic presentation of the basics of Judaism. We are confident that this book on the very sensitive topic of *tzniyus* will accomplish its sublime mission: to enable young men and women to withstand the pressures of the general society in which they live and courageously choose to conform to the eternal values of our sacred tradition.

Author's Preface

This book is a long time in coming.

I wrote the first draft nearly a decade ago, while I was working as Director of Programs for NCSY, the youth movement of the Orthodox Union. One of my projects was a question-and-answer forum called AskNCSY. Questions about *tzniyus* and other gender issues were among those most commonly asked. Not only is the topic new to beginners, even those raised in observant homes often know the *whats*, but not the *whys*.

The manuscript went through many hands and I gathered much valuable feedback but, for a variety of reasons, I placed publishing it on the metaphorical back burner. I did deliver portions of it as lectures and classes at Shabbatonim, in camps and in schools. I also made portions of it available to educators and NCSY advisors for their own use, and my research was used as the basis for at least one term paper. But I always intended to return to it, eventually.

When the first volume of my book *The Nach Yomi Companion* came out, I got a lot of, "Whatever happened to your *tzniyus* book?" Really—I got a *lot* of that. So here we are.

The motivation to write this book was simple: the book I wanted to use didn't exist. There are a number of books on this subject available, some better than others, but none of them took the approach of explaining the sources that define the practices. Current works generally focus upon the philosophies underlying *tzniyus*, or detail the laws of *tzniyus*—both important and useful—but I wanted to give people a compendium of Torah sources that showed the roots of *tzniyus*. I couldn't find one, so I had to compile it.

The intended audience for this book is the young woman who is familiar with the concepts of *tzniyus* (the *whats*), but who may not know the Torah origin of the practice to dress or act in certain ways (the *whys*). This is not intended to subtract from the philosophical reasons that may be the focal point of some other works. My book describes where God told us to do certain things, while those works speculate on the reason He may have done so. The two approaches complement one another. (I do a fair amount of philosophical speculation myself, incidental to my source-gathering.)

As I mentioned above, the original audience for this work was high school girls and it was written with that slant. I have revised the text to remove the assumption that the reader is a teen, but I think that (for good or for ill) the finished product still skews to a younger audience.

Finally, it is inevitable that people will infer matters of practical application from this book. Such is not my intent! This is not a collection of laws, it is a collection of sources. If I discuss that Orthodox girls wear skirts to the exclusion of pants or that married women cover their hair, I am addressing the reality of the situation, not mandating a list of "Thou shalts" and "Thou shalt nots." For all matters of Jewish law, please consult with a competent *halachic* authority.

Rabbi Jack Abramowitz
14 Elul, 5769

About the Language in this Book

The Gemara (*Pesachim* 3a) engages in a discussion about the euphemistic language employed by the Torah. This discussion is sparked by the statement of Rav Yehoshua ben Levi that the Torah used eight Hebrew letters more than necessary in order to avoid using a crass term, by saying "from the animals that are not clean" rather than "that are unclean."

The Gemara goes on to ask the logical question: Why should the Torah avoid the use of the word "unclean" when it uses that very word many times in other places? It answers that when a "clean" and a "crass" term are both equally appropriate, the Torah will use the nicer expression, but when the meaning may be obscured, the Torah puts the cards on the table and uses the blunter term.[1]

Most *tzniyus* books utilize the euphemistic manner of speech. When referring to women's clothes and body parts, they speak in generalities such as "inner garments" and "chest." I do not do so in this book.

First of all, I am seeking to include a population that may be younger, "hipper" or more straightforward than the intended audiences of most other such works. The principle of *chanoch lenaar al pi darko*, to educate a person in the manner best suited to him (or her) (*Mishlei* 22:6), compels me to "speak their language."

More importantly, I do not wish for my meaning to be obscured. Since many of the intended readers of this book are from backgrounds where one would not speak in this euphemistic fashion, I cannot do so if I wish to be clear. If I were to refer to "inner garments," what would I mean? Bra? Pantyhose? T-shirt? Boxer shorts? If I wish to state that it's beneath a young woman's dignity to wear fashions that display her bra strap, I'm going to have to use the word "bra." The girls who are going to read this *know* they wear bras, so why should I not make it perfectly—and appropriately—clear?

An even more important consideration is that I don't want people to think I'm speaking in euphemisms when I'm not. Later on I say that a woman is required by the Torah to cover her torso. I don't want people to think "he *means* breasts, but he's speaking euphemistically." I want it to be clear that if I *say* "torso," I *mean* "torso"—cleavage, midriff, shoulders, the whole thing.

The result is that the end product may not be palatable to those for whom it was not written. It is by no means vulgar, but some may find it too blunt. If that's you, there are, thank God, numerous existing works that will hopefully answer your questions on this crucial topic.

---

1. My friend Rabbi Gil Student shared with me an incident in which the Vilna Gaon chastised a student for speaking ill of a particular Jewish movement. "But you criticize them all the time," sputtered the incredulous student. "I only do it when necessary," the Gaon enlightened him. The message is clear: we should only speak harshly when circumstances require it, but not otherwise.

The Torah Does Too Say So!

Rabbi Yochanan said: Had the Torah not been given, we could have learned tzniyus from the cat . . . (Eiruvin 100b). It's obvious from this that *tzniyus is* from the Torah!

The most important feature of the book is that I have categorized statements from the Torah and some other major works, primarily the Talmud, on the subject of women's issues in general and *tzniyus* in particular.

The reason for this is simple. I've noticed that many girls who were not raised in homes where *tzniyus* is practiced may accept concepts such as Shabbos and kashrus, but still be skeptical when it comes to some of the "girls' rules" to which they may later become exposed. There is a certain assumption that these practices must have been made up at some medieval period by men whose motivation was at best that they were old-fashioned and at worst was to suppress women. Girls (and boys) don't see overt Torah commandments along the lines of "Thou shalt not show thy knees" and "thou shalt not go mixed swimming," so they assume that these rules must not be authentic Torah obligations.

Let me break it to you: the Torah is not always so cut and dried.

First of all, many things are explained in greater detail in the Oral Law. When Hashem gave the Torah to *Moshe Rabbeinu* (Moses) on *Har Sinai* (Mount Sinai), there were two parts, the Written Law (*Torah shebichsav*) and the Oral Law (*Torah sheb'al peh*). Despite occasional historic factions such as the Karaites and Samaritans who did not believe in the authenticity of the Oral Law, its legitimacy is obvious to anyone who has ever actually read the Torah. Here are but a few examples:

- The Torah commands us to take "the fruit of a goodly tree" as one of the four species on Succos. How do we know that means

an *esrog*? Yet nobody ever comes to *shul* waving a banana. (See *Vayikra* 23:40.)
- Men are told in the *Shema* to wear "*totafos*" on their heads. The word appears nowhere else. How do we know what *tefillin* are? (See *Devarim* 6:8.)
- The Torah commands that no one leave their place on Shabbos. Does that mean their city? Their home? Not to get out of bed? Yet we know the laws of *techum Shabbos* (Sabbath boundaries). (See *Shemos* 16:29.)
- This one's a clincher. The Torah says that when we want to eat meat, we must slaughter the animals in the way God has instructed us. But the laws of *shechita* (ritual slaughter) appear nowhere in the Torah! That's because they're in the Oral Law. (See *Devarim* 12:21.)

Here's a wild concept for you to digest: The last book of the Torah, *Devarim* (*Deuteronomy*), was a farewell speech delivered by Moshe before his death. While it is often referred to as *Mishneh Torah* (the repetition of the Torah), it contains many laws that do not appear in the first four books! That's because Hashem gave those laws to Moshe orally on Mount Sinai. Had Moshe not delivered this speech, there would not be 613 commandments in the Torah. Laws such as sending the mother bird away from the nest before taking the eggs and placing a guardrail on a flat roof would not be in the Written Torah—they would be exclusively part of the Oral Law! (For that matter, laws as basic as marriage and divorce are not given until *Devarim*. But a *kohein* was prohibited from marrying a divorcee back in *Vayikra*; clearly these procedures were already known by the people before they were recorded in the Torah.)

It goes beyond just what's in the Oral Law. Even our obligations from the Written Torah are not always explicitly laid out for us.[1] Every morning we say the "Thirteen *Midos* (methodologies) of Rabbi Yishmael" which outline the ways in which the Torah is appropriately interpreted.

So there are a lot of different ways that the Torah can teach us something. Not all of them involve saying, "Thou shalt not." In fact, most of them don't.

Almost all of the sources cited in this book are from either the Tanach (Bible) or the Talmud. For the most part I have included only sources that are of significant antiquity and are universally considered authoritative. There are some tremendously powerful statements on the subject of *tzniyus* written by later and modern *rabbanim*, but I have not included them because I wanted to demonstrate the *sources* for our practices rather than explanations after the fact.

A very few of the sources are admittedly paraphrased, but the intent is to keep their meaning in context rather than to deviate from it. The Gemara (*Kiddushin* 49a) says that anyone who translates a verse literally is actually mistranslating it. One has to consider idiom and slang. For example, the Torah frequently uses the expression that people "fell on their face." For us to use that term would be laughable. A less literal, but better, translation would be to say that the person "was greatly embarrassed." Similarly, the Gemara in *Shabbos* literally says, "Everyone knows why the bride enters the *chupah* (bridal canopy)." Someone might read that and think, "Yeah—to get married!" A less literal, but hopefully more easily understood translation is therefore employed. In this case, "everybody knows what a bride does on her wedding night" more accurately conveys the *meaning* of the Gemara, rather than the exact words.

Following each chapter, we will look at some of what the Torah has to say on the relevant issues of men and women, sexual relations and the power of what we wear. You will find that the Torah has quite a lot to say on the topics of *tzniyus* and interpersonal relationships. That's a pretty good indicator that there's something to it.

---

1. For example, there is no overt commandment prohibiting masturbation, yet we infer that God objects to the wasteful emission of semen from the fact that He struck Onan dead for wasting sperm.

What is This Tzniyus, Anyway?

Tzniyus is generally translated as "modesty" and, for our purposes, that's as good a translation as any. But that doesn't give us any real idea as to what it means.

Literally, *tzniyus* means "hidden." The meaning is that certain things are private. Not dirty or shameful, but private. Privacy is a good thing and an important thing.

In most families, the children do not know how much their parents make, but the parents each know what the other makes. That's because it's private between husband and wife. It's irrelevant whether one's father pulls down $15,000 a year or a cool million; his salary is private.

Another example: a school should not announce or post grades without permission. Whether one has a perfect 1600 SAT or a somewhat less than perfect 650, their grades are private.

Similarly, the fact that certain body parts are private does not mean that they are bad. They are, in fact, altogether good. But they are not necessarily meant for public consumption. Sometimes they're just for you. Sometimes they can be shared with other members of your gender. One can share them with a doctor if need be. And you may share them with that special someone after your wedding. Like your grades and your salary, there are some people who are privy to your private matters.

While "privacy" may be a better word than "modesty," it still doesn't give us the full scope of what we mean when we say "*tzniyus*."

The Rambam addresses the concept of problems in translation. Sometimes, he says, you need many words in one language to properly convey the meaning of a single word from another language. Just try translating "*muktza*" or "*shaatnez*." Respectively, they refer to items that may not be used (or even handled) on Shabbos and garments made of the forbidden mixture of wool and linen. These are concepts that are succinctly expressed in Hebrew, but require greater explanation in English. Even such a basic concept as "*kashrus*" may be simply translated as "dietary laws." But anyone familiar with *kashrus* knows that that phrase is insufficient to adequately convey the depth of the concept.

Similarly, *tzniyus* means more than just the secular concepts of modesty and privacy. There are major aspects of modesty and privacy to be sure, but *tzniyus* also includes an aspect of humility and an aspect of dignity. *Tzniyus* refers not only to dress, but also to speech, actions and comportment.

Tzniyus is not just about measuring how much of a girl's skin is showing. Sure, if too much skin is revealed, it's immodest, but that's only part of the picture.

Tzniyus is also not only about covering women's bodies so that men don't get "turned on" by the sight of them. *Tzniyus* isn't even just in front of boys. There is *tzniyus* in front of girls and even *tzniyus* when you're all alone. Sure, if a woman is immodestly dressed and a man does get excited by the sight, it's a problem. But, again, that's not the reason.

The reason for *tzniyus*, in my humble opinion, is that it empowers women.

Think about that for a second.

Tzniyus is not intended to repress girls or to make them subservient to men or to protect them from the imagined animal instincts of the supposedly-depraved male gender. It's to give them the power and dignity they deserve.

Form a mental image of any recent First Lady of the United States or the Queen of England. What are they wearing? Probably something very refined and modest. Dignified women wear dignified clothes. Hold that thought; we'll come back to it.

Why is it that every time what they call "art photos" (that is, nude photos) of a pop star or a beauty queen surface, it's considered newsworthy? Even if the newspapers don't print the "girlie" photos, they love to write about them and people buy the papers to read about them. Is it because the celebrity is intrinsically that much more attractive than a "regular" person? If that were the case, wouldn't the magazines have published those photos when they were first taken, instead of sticking them in the back of a filing cabinet until the model became famous?

You might say these pictures get published and the stories make the papers because we're naturally curious. Possibly, but consider these two actual (albeit dated) examples: (1) President and Mrs. Clinton were on vacation when a photographer snapped them on the beach in their bathing suits. (2) Princess Diana was photographed working out in a health club wearing a leotard. Both of these pictures were widely distributed (and in both instances, the media was criticized for publishing them).

What's the news story? The President and First Lady go swimming? Princess Di worked out? These are not particularly shocking revelations. No Pulitzers will be given for these breaking reports. And while the Clintons made for a handsome couple, they were not especially fetching in their swimsuits.

So why do people want to see these photos or even just read about them?

The reason the public likes to see celebrities in less than their proper attire is because, psychologically, it takes the mighty down a peg. What does the cliché say you should do if you're nervous while public speaking? Picture the audience in their underwear. Why should that make you feel better? Because you've lowered their esteem in your eyes. Nobody suggests picturing them as your hardest teacher, your meanest boss, or some equally intimidating authority figure; that would have the opposite effect. By mentally undressing them, you have de-powered them. That works in real life, too.

Sometimes women delude themselves into thinking that by wearing short skirts or skimpy bathing suits they are empowering themselves. "I'm independent," they think. "I dress how I like." Or even, "when I look sexy, I can get boys to do what I want."

I hate to break it to you, but no man or boy ever looked at a scantily-clad female and thought, "Now *there's* a powerful and independent woman! I'd like to vote for her!" (I don't think I need to tell you what they *are* thinking!) When a girl dresses in a revealing manner, a boy doesn't look her in the eye or listen to what she has to say. Sometimes women who dress in such a fashion even receive catcalls and other undesired attention. Now *that's* really befitting a young lady's dignity! There's really nothing quite so empowering as a construction crew yelling "hoochie mama!" But when a girl dresses in a dignified manner as befits a daughter of *Avraham Avinu* (our father Abraham), she commands the same attention one would give a First Lady or a Queen.

So far we've been discussing *tzniyus* as it pertains to girls, but one should not be misled into thinking that *tzniyus* is a "girls' *halacha*." *Tzniyus* is an important *midah* (character trait) for boys to develop, as well. The details are different, but the concepts are equally important.

It may be less problematic for a boy to appear in public in a tank top and shorts than it is for a girl, but that doesn't mean there is no boys' *tzniyus*. A swaggering manner, all machismo and testosterone, is an immodest way for a male to behave. Certain jokes and bawdy locker room talk is not *tzniyusdik* for a boy, either. They may be permitted to bare more skin than a girl (we'll discuss why that is in the next section), but that doesn't mean that they have *carte blanche* to speak, act or dress however they wish.

The "tank top and shorts" look may be permitted for a boy, but that doesn't mean it's appropriate in every situation. Not in school. Certainly not in *shul*. In fact, the only place it really *is* appropriate is on the basketball court.

Just because boys *can* occasionally get away with dressing more casually than their sisters, it doesn't mean that all males *do*. You'll never go to see a great Rabbi and find him wearing jeans and a T-shirt. It would be as beneath his dignity as wearing a bikini in public would be beneath a girl's.

All Jews have assigned uniforms. We cannot wear clothes that contain *shaatnez*, the aforementioned mixture of wool and linen in the same garment. A boy's uniform includes a *yarmulke* and *tzitzis*. A girl's uniform is clothing which we would refer to as "*tzniyusdik*." In common usage, when we speak of *tzniyus* we may often be referring to the standard of dress for a Jewish girl. This doesn't mean that *tzniyus* is only about dress or that it's only for girls. You will often, in fact usually, see the word treated as if that's exclusively what it means, but you should be aware that it encompasses so much more.

Selected Torah Sources on Tzniyus

Real Beauty Comes from Within

> *All the honor of the King's daughter is internal. Her clothing is like a gold setting (of a ring) (Tehillim 45:14).*

This may be the quintessential verse about *tzniyus* in all of Tanach—and there is so much in it!

- *King's daughter*—the Jewish girl is royalty. As a descendant of Avraham Avinu, she is deserving of treatment that elevates her, never that degrades her, God forbid!

The *Gemara, Kesubos* 17a, tells us that a king cannot choose to forego the honor due to him. If a Jewish girl is a king's daughter, she cannot "opt out" of the dignity she deserves!

- *Internal*—true beauty comes from within. Also, women do not typically take roles as public as men. We see this in the synagogue, for example. Similarly, many prominent female speakers will not lecture in front of men.
- *Gold setting*—if a girl's clothes are the setting, then the girl is the precious gem. Ask any girl with an engagement ring and she'll tell you that a stone needs an appropriate setting that complements it, not one that overshadows it or detracts from it. Similarly, a girl's clothes should complement her royal appearance, not overshadow her or, God forbid, detract from her appearance.

Modesty is Praiseworthy

> *How goodly are your tents, Yaakov, your dwelling places, Israel (Bamidbar 24:5).*

The gentile seer Bilam was hired to curse the Jews, but he praised them instead. According to Rashi, Bilam uttered this praise when he saw that the doors of the Israelites' tents were arranged so that they did not face one another. This simple modesty, that they should not see into each others' tents, was deemed praiseworthy even by a sworn enemy of the Jewish people.

To be Modest is to be with God

> *He told you what is good and what Hashem desires of you, that is to act justly, to love kindness and to walk modestly with God (Micha 6:8).*

Walking modestly is walking with God. (Contrast with *Yeshaya* 3:16, "the girls of Israel have become full of themselves . . . walking with deliberate steps.")

Tzniyus Keeps Hashem Dwelling Among Us

> *Your camp must be holy and there must not be seen in you anything inappropriate (literally: anything naked) so that God will not turn away from you (Devarim 23:15).*

Keeping it Private is Godly

> *The glory of Hashem is in the hidden things, while the glory of (human) kings is to reveal things (Mishlei 25:2).*

When a human king does something great, everybody has to know about it. This is not the case with God. God's greatest works, the act of Creation and the vision of the Chariot in *sefer Yechezkel* (the Book of Ezekiel), are the acts whose meanings are the most hidden. Similarly, we have certain personal (physical) attributes which are greater glory to ourselves to keep private. (This is also a glory to God because "the glory of Hashem is in the hidden things.")

Using Our Bodies for God

> *My soul desires and longs for the courtyards of Hashem, my heart and flesh will praise the living God (Tehillim 84:3).*

Everyone understands that we must serve Hashem with our hearts and our souls. What is not so obvious is that we must also serve him with our flesh, as well.

Taking the Extra Step

> *Regarding women's pools where the lifeguard is a man . . . if it is permitted for a frum woman to swim there, since the place is designated for women's swimming, it is like her house and not a place of promiscuity (to appear less than fully clothed) since the man is not there for promiscuity, but to do his job . . . and he would certainly get in trouble if he gave in to his passions instead of doing his job . . . nevertheless, a God-fearing woman shouldn't swim there . . .* (Igros Moshe Even HaEzer IV, 62, 1)

I hesitate to quote from the *Igros Moshe* because people have a disturbing tendency to make decisions in their own lives based upon answers given in *teshuvos* (responsa). Nevertheless, Rav Moshe made a very important point in this *teshuva*: just because something *may* be done, it doesn't necessarily mean that it *should* be done!

Overdressing Creates Problems

> *If the prideful (among Jews) would disappear, those who cause us suffering would disappear* (Shabbos 139a).

Rashi explains prideful to include dressing pretentiously.

Al Chait

> **For the sin we committed before you in sexual matters (gilui arayos).*
> **For the sin we committed before you through consensual promiscuity (v'idas z'nus).*
> **For the sin we committed before you with the impurity of our lips (tumas s'fasaim).*
> **For the sin we committed before you through misuse of our vision (shikur ayin).*
> (*Yomim Noraim* service)

Not to Entice

> *Don't curse the deaf or put an obstacle in front of the blind and you shall fear your God—I am Hashem* (Vayikra 19:14).

It is widely known that "putting an obstacle in front of the blind" doesn't just mean in the literal sense. It includes not enticing people into making bad moves or committing sins. While the purpose of *tzniyus* is *not* to keep women from enticing men into lustful thoughts or actions, women must be aware that it may be an unintentional consequence of wearing inappropriate clothes. They may accidentally be violating the commandment of *lifnei iver* (misleading others) by appearing in public scantily clad.

> *Rabbi Yochanan says we learned fear of sin from a young girl . . . Rabbi Yochanan heard a girl bow down in prayer and say, "Master of the Universe, you created Heaven and Hell, righteous and wicked. May it be Your will that no man be enticed into sin through me"* (Sotah 22a).

Selected Torah Sources on the Power of the Human Body

Hair

> *When you bring (the captive woman—a prisoner of war) into your home, you shall shave her head and let her nails grow* (Devarim 21:12).

The Ibn Ezra explains that the reason her head is shaved is to make her less attractive to her captor. A woman's hair, as our own experience tells us, is attractive to a man. The Torah recognizes this reality.

> *You are beautiful, my love, you are beautiful. Your eyes are like doves, your hair inside your kerchief is like a flock of goats that stream down from Mount Gilad* (Shir HaShirim 4:1).

The Midrash explains this verse to say that well-kempt hair, neatly tied back is a flattering look for women.

> *Rav Sheshes says a woman's hair is a sexually-attractive part of her, based upon the verse "your hair is like a flock of goats"* (Brachos 24a).

The analogy of a flock of goats may be lost on our modern audience, but the intent is flowing, cascading down like a flock of goats down a mountain. The Talmud is interpreting the previously-quoted verse from *Shir HaShirim*.

> *Rav Shimon ben Menasia says that the verse "Hashem built the rib (into a woman)" means that God braided Chava's (Eve's) hair before he brought her to Adam. In seaside towns braiding is called "building"* (*Brachos* 61a, *Shabbos* 95a, et al).

Why would this even be necessary? After all, Chava was (a) the only woman in the world and (b) naked, so Adam presumably would have been attracted to her regardless of how her hair looked! Nevertheless, Hashem deemed it appropriate and important to beautify Chava's hair before bringing her to Adam.

> *Ohn ben Peles was saved by his wife. She said, "What difference does it make to you whether Moshe remains in charge or Korach becomes the leader? Either way you remain a follower!" . . . She got him drunk and lay him down inside the tent. She then sat down at the entrance and uncovered her hair so that whoever came to get Ohn would turn around* (*Sanhedrin* 109b-110a).

Ohn was scheduled to take part in Korach's uprising, but his wife saved him from that folly. While Korach's followers were rebellious, they were not so base as to intrude on a lady who was not properly attired. Ohn's wife knew that only a cad would stay and talk with a lady who was not dressed and she used that to get Korach's men to depart. The Talmud takes for granted that uncovered hair in a married woman considered a state of undress.

The Neck

> *Your neck is like the Tower of David, built like an ornament . . .*
> (*Shir HaShirim* 4:4).

Rashi explains that an upright posture is attractive in a woman. He also explains that the neck is like an ornament in that it is beautiful and everybody gazes at it.

Legs

> Uncover your arms, lift up your dress and uncover your legs and cross the rivers. Your nakedness will be exposed and your shame will be seen. I will take revenge and no man will hold me back (*Yeshaya* 47:2-3).

This verse is explained by the Gemara as follows:

> Rav Chisda says a woman's thigh is sexual based upon the verse "uncover your leg" which is followed by "your nakedness will be exposed" (*Brachos* 24a).

We extrapolate that the thigh is considered an *ervah* (a private part of the body), since the Torah calls uncovering the leg "nakedness."

Breasts

Judaism is perceived by many as being prudish, but nothing could be further from the truth. If anything, Judaism has a very realistic outlook on human sexuality. The breasts, a natural part of the human body, are an unnatural source of obsession in American culture. The Torah acknowledges that they have a quality of attraction, but more importantly, a holy purpose.

> Rav Yossi the son of Rav Chanina says he (the prophet Elisha) was holy, but his servant was not holy. It says, "And Gechazi came near to push her away." Rav Yossi the son of Chanina says he grabbed her by the pride of her beauty (*Brachos* 10b).

The Gemara uses the awkward expression "the pride of her beauty" (*hod yafeha*) as a play on words with the word *l'hadfa*, to push her. Rashi explains that the pride of a woman's beauty refers to the breasts. The Gemara clearly expects that readers would understand from context that breasts are the "pride of a woman's beauty." We are not naïve or oblivious to their power of attraction, but that is not their importance, as seen in the following examples.

> *My soul praises Hashem and will not forget all His benefits (Tehillim 103:2).*

An alternative reading is suggested by the word *gemulav* (His benefits), which is related to the word *gamal*, to wean. This alternate reading is: My soul praises Hashem that He does not forget all those who nurse. The relationship of these two words is utilized by the Gemara in the following example:

> *When David nursed from his mother's breast, he composed the psalm "my soul praises Hashem and will not forget all His benefits." To what benefit does this refer? Rav Abahu says that He placed the breasts at the heart, which is the place of understanding. Why did He do this? Rav Yehuda says so that when the baby sucks it will not be staring at the genitals (Brachos 10a).*

Human anatomy is radically different from other mammals. Hashem specifically designed humans so that nursing is a spiritually uplifting experience for mother and child and does not expose the baby to "unclean" sights.

> *Your two breasts are like two fawns, twins of a gazelle who graze among the roses (Shir HaShirim 4:5)*

Rashi gives two explanations for this verse. First, the breasts refer to Moshe and Aharon who "nursed" the Jewish people in its infancy and are "twins" in greatness. Alternatively, it refers to the *luchos* (Tablets) which are "twins" with five commandments on each.

You will note that it is not disrespectful to Moshe and Aharon or to the Torah to be compared to a woman's breasts. Rather than being a source of titillation as in countless teen comedies, the breasts have an important and holy purpose. They forge the bond between mother and child and nourish the next generation.

Selected Torah Sources on the Power of Clothing

The Importance of Clothes

> *The eyes of both (Adam and Chava) were opened and they realized that they were naked, so they sewed together fig leaves and made themselves loincloths (Bereishis 3:7).*

Rashi explains that this doesn't mean that they literally saw that they were naked; it means that, having gained wisdom, they understood what it meant to be naked. After all, even a blind person knows whether or not he's wearing clothes!

> *God made garments of skin for Adam and his wife and He dressed them (Bereishis 3:21).*

These may have been garments of leather or, according to Rashi, possibly of a soft wool.[1] The *Gemara* (*Sotah* 14a) uses this verse to praise Hashem that the Torah opens with *chesed* (acts of kindness) and closes with *chesed*. It closes with Hashem burying Moshe and it opens with Hashem clothing Adam and Chava. The praise is not that Hashem created the world but that He clothed the naked.

> *Blessed are you, Hashem our God, King of the universe, who clothes the naked* (Morning blessings).

To Wear Suitable Clothes

> *Strength and dignity are her clothing and she rejoices until the last day (Mishlei 31:25).*

Alternatively, "she wears clothes of strength and dignity." These words are probably familiar to you from *Eishes Chayil*. (That allegorical song of praise for Jewish women is actually taken from this chapter of *Mishlei*.) In it, one can find the secret to building a *bayis ne'eman b'Yisroel* (a true Jewish home). The "woman of valor" rejoices until her last day because she is assured of the good name she will have earned by the time her end comes.

Shir HaShirim Rabbah (2:10), commenting on the verse in *Tehillim* 29 ("Hashem will give strength to His nation") explains that there is no "strength" except Torah. If strength can only mean Torah, and strength and dignity are the Jewish woman's clothing, then most important things one can wrap around oneself each day are words of Torah.

> *These are examples of vows that afflict the soul (that a husband may therefore annul for his wife): not to eat meat, not to drink wine and not to wear colorful clothes (Kesubos 71a-71b).*

Rashi says the husband can annul a vow not to wear colorful clothes because it is an embarrassment for the woman and wearing drab clothes will make her unattractive to her husband.

The Power of Clothes

> *Potiphar's wife tried to seduce Yosef with words. The clothes she wore for him in the morning she did not wear for him in the evening and the clothes she wore for him in the evening she did not wear for him in the morning (Yoma 35b).*

An experienced seductress, Potiphar's wife knew that frequent changes of clothing would get a man to notice her. It's important to note that she didn't just wear a lot of different clothes, she wore them "for" Yosef.

> *The Torah says, "And you shall gird Aharon and his sons in belts and put their turbans on their heads and they will have the priesthood as an eternal statute." We learn from this that they possess the priesthood when they are wearing their priestly garments, but that they do not have the priesthood when they are not wearing their priestly garments (Zevachim 17b).*

Of course a *kohein* is still a *kohein* even if he's not dressed in his "uniform," but *Tosfos* explains that if he does the service without his priestly clothes, he's considered a *zar* (non-*kohein*) and is liable to the death penalty. Similarly, a Jew who dresses "out of uniform" is still a Jew, but how much of his holiness has he or she divested by dressing inappropriately?

> Who doesn't know that fancy embroidered clothes make one haughty and border on promiscuous behavior, in addition to jealousy, lust and oppression which grab hold of anything a person finds desirable? (*Mesillas Yesharim* 13).

> There are two things that accustom a person to humility—habit and thought. Habit means that a person gradually accustoms himself to acting with humbleness—sitting in lesser places, walking at the end of the group and wearing modest clothes, namely those that are honorable but not showy (*Mesillas Yesharim* 23).

Clothes Bestow Honor

> "Under his honor will be kindled a burning like the burning of fire." What does it mean under his honor? Their bodies were burned inside and their clothes remained on the outside because the honor of a person is in his clothes. (*Shemos Rabbah* 18:5)

The Midrash continues: "Why did their clothes remain? Because they were descendants of Shem." This was a reward because Shem clothed his father Noach.

(The *Etz Yosef* cross-references this Midrash with the Gemara in *Shabbos* 113a, so we shall do likewise. See the section "Shabbos Clothes," below.)

The Right Clothes Can Save You

> "I will extract you, I will save you, I will redeem you and I will take you"—(these four terms of redemption) correspond to four merits that B'nei Yisroel possessed, namely that (during their stay in Egypt) they did not change their language, they did not change their style of dress, they did not reveal each others' secrets (to the authorities)... and they did not cease performing bris milah (*Psiksa Zutrasa*, *Shemos* 6:6).

> "They became a distinct nation there"—Their clothes and food were different from those of the Egyptians... they were distinct and visible in their religion and practices until it became clear that they were a nation in their own right... this teaches that

> *B'nei Yisroel were recognizable through their clothes as it says (in the Psiksa Zutrsa, quoted above) that they did not change their clothes or their language (Baalei Tosfos Haggadah).*[2]

The Wrong Clothes Can Betray You

> *Rav Zeira interpreted the verse, "He smelled the smell of his clothes." Do not read it as "begadav" (his clothes), but as "bogadav" (his traitors) (Sanhedrin 57a).*

The context of this quote is not relevant to *tzniyus*; it is brought to demonstrate the linguistic relationship of the Hebrew words for clothes and traitor. Another word for clothes, *levush*, is related to the words *lo busha*, will not embarrass. Your choice of clothes can betray you, or it can prevent embarrassment.

While we're on the subject of linguistics, the word for promiscuity, *pritzus*, comes from the expression *poretz geder*, to breach the fence, meaning to behave in a fashion that breaks down the accepted practices of Jewish society.

See-Through Clothes are Unacceptable

> *It was said of Rabbi Elazar ben Harsom that his mother made him a robe worth 20,000 mina, but his fellow kohanim did not let him wear it because he looked naked in it. But how could it be transparent when the clothes of the kohanim were made of six-ply thread? Abaye explained that it was like seeing wine through the bottle (Yuma 35b).*

Rashi clarifies that, just as you can see the color of the wine through a thick glass bottle, the color of the *kohein*'s flesh was visible through the translucent robe. This was still considered "looking naked."

There's a Reason it's Called "Underwear"

> *Kimchis had seven sons, all of whom served as Kohein Gadol (High Priest) at some point. The Rabbis sent a messenger who asked her what merit she possessed. She answered, "I promise that the beams of my house did not see the hair of my head or the hem of my undergarment in my whole life. They responded that*

most flour (kemach) is coarse but that the flour of Kimchis is fine (Yerushalmi Megilla 1:10).

The Rabbis' response is a praise based upon a play on Kimchis' name and the word *kemach,* meaning flour. Compare this story with the more familiar version appearing in the Talmud Bavli (see page 92). In the Bavli, Kimchis only speaks of her hair and the Rabbis reject her theory. This version includes not revealing her underwear and the Rabbis accept her opinion. This is something to think about when considering fashions that display bra straps and elastic waistbands.

Prioritizing One's Appearance

Grace is false and beauty is empty; a woman who fears God is the one who will be praised (Mishlei 31:30).

It may be important to take pride in one's appearance, but one must also keep in mind the truly important things in life.

Listen, daughter, and see, so bend your ear . . . The King will desire your beauty because he is your Master and you bow before Him (Tehillim 45:12).

When does God (the King) appreciate one's beauty? When we acknowledge Him as the Master of the world and do His will, He appreciates the beauty of our actions.

Shabbos Clothes

"And you should honor Shabbos, not doing things in your usual way." This verse means that we should honor Shabbos with clothes that are not like our weekday clothes. Similar to this, Rav Yochanan called his clothes "the ones that honor" (Shabbos 113a).

It's important to dress better on Shabbos than one might during the week. But clothes which are appropriate for Shabbos might be too flashy for other occasions. You wouldn't go to work or school dressed the same as you would for a wedding! Similarly, there should be a distinction between our regular clothes and Shabbos clothes.

> *Rav Huna says that if one has a change of clothes for Shabbos, he should change. If not, he should wear his clothes lower to make them appear longer. (Rashi says that this was the style favored by men of leisure.) Rav Safra objected, "doesn't this appear to be overly fashion-conscious?" Since he only does it on Shabbos, it is obvious that he isn't doing it to be fashionable (Shabbos 113a).*

The point of dressing up is to honor Shabbos, and thereby Hashem, not to be fashionable. If anything, being overly concerned with fashion on a daily basis was not seen as a positive trait.

> *"Wash yourself, anoint yourself and put your clothes on." Rabbi Elazar says that this verse refers to Shabbos clothes (Shabbos 113b).*

> *How do we learn from the Torah to change clothes as a sign of honor? Because it says, "Take off your clothes and put on other clothes" (Shabbos 114a).*

Immodest Garments

> *The former generations used to risk their lives to sanctify God's name, but we do not risk our lives to sanctify God's name. Rav Ada bar Ahaba saw a non-Jewish woman in the street wearing a red cloak. Thinking she was Jewish, he tore it from her. When it was discovered that she was not Jewish, he was fined 400 zuz (Brachos 20a).*

People often misinterpret this Gemara. They imagine that the woman must have been wearing an immodest garment like a miniskirt or a tank top. If that were the case and he tore it off her, wouldn't that have been *more* immodest? In reality, she was wearing an immodest outer garment, like a flashy coat. Such garments are meant solely to attract attention to one's physicality and are immodest even if one is otherwise completely covered.

1. Some suggest that this means that Hashem caused the "protective skins" over the genitalia to grow, namely the male foreskin and the female hymen (*Maaseh Hashem*, quoted by Rabbi Aryeh Kaplan).
2. Many sources refer to a "well-known Midrash" that *B'nei Yisroel* merited redemption from Egypt because of three things: that they did not alter their style of dress, their names or their language. None of these sources cite the origin of this "well-known Midrash." When my research failed to turn it up, I turned to colleagues who also were unable to locate this piece. It appears to be a later synthesis of ideas from two separate Midrashim. I have cited two sources as similar to the familiar (albeit apparently misquoted) one as I was able to find.

    In Salomon Buber's notes to *Pesikta D'Rav Kahana*, he notes that "The familiar statement that (the Jews) did not change their style of dress is not recorded in any place." (Cited by *Torah Sheleima* 8:3, among others.)

The Difference

It bothers—I mean *really* bothers—some girls that there are different rules for girls and for boys. They also perceive the rules that apply to them as being more stringent than the boys' rules. As we will soon see, the perception of stringency depends on which side of the gender fence you are on.

Before we discuss that, let us analyze why there are different standards of *tzniyus* for boys and for girls.

Here's a harsh fact of life. It's better you learn it now:

Boys and girls are different.

I know this comes as a shock to you but it's about time you were told.

How are boys and girls different? In almost every conceivable way. Let's examine a few of them.

Intellectually. Studies have shown again and again that girls typically do better in verbal subjects such as English and Social Studies, as well as on the verbal section of the SAT. Boys are generally stronger in math and science and on the math section of the SAT.[1] (Let us leave aside debates as to whether this is based on inherent differences or biases in teaching methodologies as outside the scope of this work and just focus on the reality that, for whatever reason, there is a difference.)

Emotionally. Forget all the Mars and Venus stuff; let's take something simple like renting a movie. You go to Blockbuster on a Saturday night and see a group of three women browsing together. Elsewhere in the store are three men. If you had to bet, which group would you say is more likely to go home with the blockbuster action film and which with the romantic comedy? Again, it's a generalization, but if you had to bet, you know how you'd wager.

Physically. (Duh.) Just go into any pharmacy and ask to see the women's personal hygiene products. You'll find two aisles packed with every conceivable item and a few inconceivable ones. Now ask for men's personal hygiene items. You'll eventually find half a shelf tucked away somewhere in the back of the store with scattered items that have been gathering dust since the Carter administration. This is not because men lack hygiene (which may or may not be the case); it is because of different biological necessities.

Of course, some of these examples may be overly-simplified, but the point is clear:

Males ≠ Females

So, working under the premise that men and women have different intellectual, emotional and physical predispositions, let's take a quiz. Which would you assume to be more likely?

____ Men and women have the same spiritual needs.

____ Men and women have different spiritual needs.

If you guessed that men and women have different spiritual needs, you're right! The Torah recognizes that men and women are different and Hashem, in His infinite wisdom, gave them many different obligations, designed to play to each gender's spiritual strengths. The most obvious, or at least the most talked about, is that women are exempt from *mitzvos asei she'hazman grama*, positive time-bound commandments (see *Kiddushin* 29a, *et al*).

There are two types of *mitzvos*, *mitzvos asei* ("Thou shalts") and *mitzvos lo sa'asei* ("Thou shalt nots"). Women are obligated in *mitzvos lo sa'asei* (not to kill, not to steal, not to eat pork) the same as men.

Mitzvos asei are sub-categorized into *mitzvos asei she'hazman grama* and *mitzvos asei she'ain hazman grama*. The former are *mitzvos* which are to be performed only at certain specified times (such as putting on *tefillin* on weekdays or taking a *lulav* on Succos), while the latter are in effect all the time (such as having a *mezuzah* on your door). With the exception of a few special cases, women are exempt from the positive, time-bound *mitzvos*. (There are only a handful of these *mitzvos* to begin with; there are more negative *mitzvos* than positive ones and most of the positive ones are in effect at all times.)

These differences do not make one gender intrinsically better or worse; they're just different. Which are better, dogs or cats? Hamburgers or frankfurters? The Beatles or the Rolling Stones? My personal preferences for dogs, hamburgers and the Beatles do not make them objectively "better." Similarly, the fact that men and women do not have the same religious requirements does not make either gender superior. It just reflects their different personal spiritual needs and the role that each gender plays within the greater picture of *klal Yisroel* (the Jewish people). The same is true for *mitzvos* unique to Kohanim, Leviim, first-born males, and other populations with occasionally unique assignments.

That having been said, it should not surprise us that men and women have different standards for *tzniyus*. They are different. Their bodies are different. The effect that their bodies can have on themselves and others, of both genders, is different. Accordingly, the standard of *tzniyus* is different.

It's not old-fashioned or sexist to think that. We see it in our society. In the summer, acceptable women's business may attire include miniskirts and sleeveless tops. ("Acceptable" in the business world, that is, not in *halacha*.) Men have the same jackets and ties that they wear year-round. Nobody wants to see their hairy legs or armpits.

At weddings, women wear a wide array of low-cut, slit, sleeveless, backless, strapless, whatever-less dresses. (Again, conforming to society, not *halacha*.) Men? Tux, tux, tux.

Judaism is not unique in having a different standard of dress for men and women. Secular society has it, too. Except that American culture says, "If you've got it, flaunt it." Judaism says, "If you've got it, revere it. Elevate it. Make it holy."

What did I mean when I said, a few paragraphs back, that "the effect that their bodies can have on themselves and others, of both genders, is different?" That wasn't implying that women are sexually stimulating to both men and women but they are attractive to both genders. Again, look at popular culture. If you want to sell a magazine to men—I don't care if it's *Playboy* or *Esquire*—there's got to be an attractive woman on the cover. What do you think the best-selling issue of *Sports Illustrated* is every year? The Super Bowl issue? Nope, it's the swimsuit issue. (And swimsuits aren't even a sport, per se!) Even if it's a car magazine, the model may be sprawled over the hood of an SUV, but there *will* be a woman on display.

What about women's magazines? Again, it could be *Elle, Vogue* or *Ladies' Home Journal,* but there's a woman on the cover. That's because women sell to both men and women. Women notice other women more than men notice other men. Men spend precious little time at formal gatherings discussing other men's outfits.

Society understands it. A woman is a thing of beauty. Even if she's having a bad hair day. Even if she feels she has to lose a few pounds. Yes, even if she's not a supermodel, a woman has tremendous power. The challenge is to understand how to channel it.

Finally, I said that I'd explain how the perception of stringency in *mitzvos* depends upon which side of the gender barrier one is on. Let's take three examples: *minyan* (praying with a quorum of ten), *tzitzis* (a fringed garment) and *kol isha* (the prohibition of a woman singing in the presence of men). (The "arguments" presented by the male and female protagonists below are not cogent, well-thought out points. They are representative of the knee-jerk reaction that both genders occasionally have to perceived inequities based on different *halachic* requirements.)

Minyan:

She: No fair! How come I can't count in a *minyan*? It's so sexist!
He: No fair! Why do I have to get up early to go to *shul* while she can sleep in and *daven* at home?

Tzitzis:

She: Why can't I wear *tzitzis*? It's so sexist!
He: Why do I have to wear *tzitzis*? It's boiling out!

Kol Isha:

She: Why do I have to refrain from singing just because there are men here? That's so sexist!
He: My mother and sister are going to a Broadway show, but I can't go because it's a musical!

Who has it tougher? Objectively, neither one. Each gender has different rules and responsibilities, challenges and obstacles, tests and triumphs. (I have demonstrated in a hopefully tongue-in-cheek fashion that young ladies often ascribe these differences to "sexism" on the part of the Rabbis of earlier generations, *chas v'shalom*. Young men obviously can make no such complaint, but they do occasionally find their obligations as "inequitable" as their sisters.)

So there you have it. Males and females are different. Everybody knows it and to act otherwise would be disingenuous. For Judaism to have one standard for everybody, regardless of gender, would not fulfill everyone's spiritual needs or provide the Jewish people with the full, rich tapestry of *mitzvos*. Those who think that women lack "equality" in Judaism because of these differences are sometimes naïve, occasionally they have an agenda, but usually they are trying to look at Torah through the perspective of secular society. Because "equality" in the secular world means that women can do everything that men can, and vice versa, they posit that Judaism's differing practices for men and women must be a sign of inequality. Nothing could be farther from the truth

Hashem knows that men and women are different and He gave the Torah accordingly. Women acting like men does not make the genders equal. Men have certain unique *mitzvos* and so do women (as do Kohanim, the King, and men whose brothers die leaving childless widows, among others). Everybody has their own job to do and doing it with a full heart to serve our Creator helps us grow to be better people. Women being the best women they can be and men being the best men they can be—*that* makes the genders equal!

---

1. Actually, while boys do better on math than they do on verbal, and while girls do better on verbal than they do on math, boys do better than girls on *both* parts of the SAT! There are literally dozens of sources to back up that statement, including *Digest of Education Statistics 2000, 1999 Profile of College-Bound Seniors—Pennsylvania Report*, and the study of scores for entering freshmen at Francis Marion University in South Carolina from 1996-2001. In each of these, the boys did better on math than on verbal, the girls did better on verbal than on math, and the boys did better than the girls on both.

However, for some reason, the SAT gender gap may be closing. In 1972, men scored an average of 46 points higher than women on the SAT; by 1996, that had dropped to a difference of 39 points. This may not seem like much, but this was *before* conscious efforts were made to eliminate potential gender bias. (Source: Women's Equity Resource Center.)

Selected Torah Sources on Men and Women

Different Approaches for Men and Women

> *And Moshe went up (to speak) with God and God called to him from the mountain saying, "This is what you shall say to the house of Jacob and speak to the children of Israel" (Shemos 19:3).*

Rashi explains that the words "*Bais Yaakov*" (house of Jacob) refer to the women, while "*B'nei Yisroel*" (children of Israel) refers to the men. (Many girls' schools are called *Bais Yaakovs* based upon this verse.) Rashi further explains the difference in the choice of verbs. For the women the Torah uses the word "*tomar*" (infinitive: *leimor*) meaning to say something gently. For the men it says "*tageid*" (infinitive: *l'hagid*) meaning to speak harshly. As discussed in the previous chapter, natural differences between men and women call for different approaches.

Inherent Modesty of Woman

> *Hashem said, "I will not create woman from the head so that she will not be haughty, not from the eye so that she will not be flirtatious, not from the ear that she should not eavesdrop, not from the mouth so that she should not gossip, not from the heart so she should not be argumentative, not from the hand so that she shouldn't be thievish, not from the leg so that she shouldn't run around. Rather, I will create her from the most modest place of a man because even when a man is naked that place is covered." And for every limb He created in her, Hashem said, "Be modest." (Bereishis Rabbah 18:3)*

The Midrash goes on to be ironic by giving examples from Tanach in which various women still eavesdropped, stole, etc., despite not being created from those parts. All I can say is that if women have the capacity for those negative traits which stem from the rejected parts, they certainly have the capacity for *tzniyus*, the attribute of the rib, which was actually their template!

Women Get Extra Consideration

> *For any deceased relative, even if one is wearing ten layers, he only tears the top layer; for the father or the mother one must tear all of them . . . Rab Shimon ben Elazar says a woman tears her inner garment first, turns it around, then tears her outer garment . . . for any deceased relative, one may pin the rip after seven days and repair the rip after thirty days; for the father or mother one may pin it after thirty days and never repair it. A woman may pin it immediately because of the honor due to her (Moed Katan 22b).*

Even when it comes to something as serious as tearing *keriah* during a period of mourning, we do not overlook the modesty of a woman and the respect she deserves. It would be counter to a woman's honor to bare her chest or publicly reveal her undergarments, even in mourning for a parent, God forbid.

> *A man is stoned with a loin cloth in front only; a woman is covered in front and behind. This is the opinion or Rabbi Yehuda. The Sages say that a man is stoned naked but a woman is not stoned naked (Mishna Sanhedrin 6:3).*

Even more extreme than the case of mourning is the case where one has been sentenced to death. There is a difference of opinion in the Gemara regarding which is preferable—to have a quicker, more painless death naked or a slightly more lingering execution clothed (since clothing cushions the stoning, however slightly). In either case, a woman receives more coverage than a man, even at the time of an execution!

Community Standards

When I was in high school, my friend Aviva, who was a few grades ahead of me, came back from a year of study in Israel. The summer was hot and humid (as it tends to be) and she complained of the relative discomfort of wearing stockings in the summer, a practice which was still new to her.

"So why wear them?" I asked.

"You have to wear stockings in a place where it is the *minhag* (custom)," she explained.

"And is it the custom on Long Island?" I inquired.

"It's the custom *everywhere*," she informed me.

The logic of that proposition eluded me then as it eludes me now, but it introduces an important principle, that of community standards. Not everything is black or white. There is some leeway in one's practice, but what is acceptable in one place may not be acceptable in another.

When it comes to *tzniyus*, there are three levels of *ervah*, private areas. Parts of the body that are Biblically-required to be covered include a woman's entire torso, a married woman's hair and the genitals of both genders. Parts that are Rabbinically-required to be covered include areas such as a girl's upper arm. The necessity to cover some other body parts, such as the calf of the leg, and the acceptable methods of covering certain parts, may fall into categories of accepted practice in a given community.

Let's take Aviva's stockings as a perfect example. In some communities, the accepted practice is to wear opaque stockings with seams in the back. In other communities the practice is to wear regular tights (not with seams), but only opaque (so that one will not mistake flesh colored pantyhose for bare skin). Still other communities accept flesh colored tights, others accept knee socks, and still others permit ankle socks. And, of course, there are those whose practice is to wear no lower leg, ankle or foot covering whatsoever.

The source of discrepancy is that when a community holds a certain standard, they do not typically believe that they are following a *chumrah* (stringency in Jewish law). They usually believe that their practice reflects the actual *halacha* and they have sources to support their opinions.

This does not undermine the integrity of any community's practice. Communities differ in many accepted practices. Let's look at some examples of accepted differences in community practices:

- *Matzah* which has been soaked in water, such as is used to make matzah balls, is called *gebrukhts*. Some communities eat *gebrukhts* on Pesach, while others do not.
- Every Jewish male agrees that they have to make a division between the upper part and the lower part of their bodies when they *daven*[1] and that they are not permitted to shave the temples of their heads[2], but only some wear a special belt called a *gartel* designated for *davening* and grow their *payes* (sidelocks) long.

So who's right? All of them, as long as they base their opinions on accepted Torah opinions, the word of the Torah as explained by the Rabbis. Who's wrong? Any of them when practiced without the approval of Torah authority for personal or political motivations.

Similarly, there are many differences in community practice when it comes to issues of *tzniyus*. In some communities, women only cover their hair with a *tichel* (head scarf). Others permit a *shaitel* (wig). Still others may only permit a *shaitel* to be worn if there is a hat on top. Skirt lengths, sleeve lengths, and other issues differ from community to community.

Of course, not every community has adopted a universal standard. In those cases, one's practice can reflect affinity with a given population. Generally speaking, when a man wears a white knit *kippah* or a black hat, he is making a statement about his religious philosophy. It may be unintentional, but a statement is being made nonetheless. Similarly, the choices a girl makes for herself will make a statement—intentional or unintentional—about where she sees herself in the Jewish community.

Community standards do not only affect how much skin one is allowed to expose. Let's take the example of body piercing. It is not prohibited for a Jewish girl to pierce her ears, as is evident from the fact that many of the most religious communities endorse the practice. But what about piercing other parts? Nowadays it is not uncommon for young people of both genders to pierce their noses, lips, tongues, eyebrows, navels, nipples and genitals. If piercing is permitted in concept, may someone pierce a part of the body other than their ears?

Piercing is not overtly prohibited by the Torah. There is no law, "Thou shalt not pierce thy tongue." There is, however, the issue of *b'chukoseihem lo selieichu*, that we are not allowed to copy the practices of the nations among whom we live (*Vayikra* 18:3). If the Jewish community doesn't accept it, we are not allowed to do it.

Nose piercing may not only have once been permitted, it was apparently practiced in Biblical times. One of the gifts which Eliezer gave to Rivka when he betrothed her to Yitzchak was a *nezem* (nose ring). Despite this, it is not currently accepted in *frum* communities. For a girl in such a community to pierce her nose and rely upon the fact that *Rivka Imeinu* (our foremother Rebecca) may have done so is to flaunt the accepted practice of the Jewish people. Is it intrinsically prohibited? Presumably not, if Rivka's nose was pierced. But is it considered acceptable today? Definitely not. And to do so would therefore violate *b'chukoseihem*. (Similarly it is not accepted in Jewish communities for boys even to pierce their ears.)

If you're thinking of piercing any other parts of your face or anything below the neck, you can forget that altogether. You don't even have Rivka to rely upon (and, as we stated, her example is not enough to permit piercing noses nowadays, anyway). Tattooing, by the way, *is* overtly prohibited by to the Torah. But don't freak out if you're on your way to becoming more observant and you're already pierced or tattooed. If that's your case you have presumably also eaten *treif* (non-kosher food) and violated Shabbos at some point. Some people who become religious aren't virgins before marriage. If God can love and accept people despite those things in their past, He can certainly handle the hole through your navel or the rose on your shoulder.[3] You shouldn't let these minor cosmetic alterations psychologically impede your religious growth, but you also shouldn't justify expanding your canvas.

Let's get back to standards of dress that may or may not be acceptable in different Torah communities. Assuming that one does not live in a homogenous community with a clear-cut practice, how does a young lady decide the proper method of dress for herself?

The trick is for a girl to investigate honestly which Torah authorities endorse which practices and, in consultation with her teachers or role models, to choose based on that. She should not automatically leap for the most lenient practice. For a girl to pick a significant way of her life based solely on the path of least resistance is to do herself a grave disservice. (Although she may legitimately choose a more lenient practice after an honest evaluation of the options.) Should someone default to the least Shabbos possible or the minimum amount of *kashrus*? Just as someone should strive to keep the best Shabbos and the best *kashrus*, people should want to keep the best *tzniyus* possible. What that is may not be the same for everybody.

Keeping the best *tzniyus* does *not* mean going straight for the most stringent opinion. That's no more preferable than going straight for the most lenient position. The *Gemara* in *Chulin* (43b-44a) says that a person who keeps all leniencies is a *rasha* (wicked), while one who keeps every stringency is a fool. So what is one to do?

The answer is simple. Consult with Rabbis, teachers and women whom you admire and aspire to be like. Don't pick and choose like you would from a menu; consistently follow one approach. Make an honest investigation of the issues and find out what the Torah says.

One of the most unusual phenomena I have seen in *tzniyus* comes up regarding many girls who have strong backgrounds in Jewish education and who wear pants. I'm not going to tell you that you cannot wear pants, but in all my experience, not one of these girls who keeps Shabbos and *kashrus* can tell me who permits it. They know that many women only wear skirts and dresses. They know that they may not wear pants in *shul* and in their schools. They are well aware that, for some reason, a lot of religious women just don't wear pants.

So why do *they* wear pants? They don't know. They've seen it done, so it must be okay. But so far none of them have ever presented me with a Torah opinion. These girls—who care about their Judaism—cannot tell you why they wear pants. They know that there is a concept that women do not wear pants, but they don't know where it comes from or why they themselves do not follow it. When making choices, it is *imperative* to know what the options actually are!

Anyone reading this is certainly old enough to make intelligent choices. But one can only make an intelligent choice if one knows what the options are! Consult with your rabbis and role models, especially women whom you would like to emulate. The Mishna in *Avos* 1:6 tells us to acquire a teacher. This person will help you develop an approach that is both "kosher" and suits your lifestyle.

1. *Orach Chaim* 91:2, *Mishna Brurah* 91:5
2. *Vayikra* 19:27
3. One Rav who reviewed this manuscript put it this way: *Teshuva*—repentance—wipes out the act, even though the mark remains.

Selected Torah Sources on Community Standards

The Importance of "Jewish Style"

> *If the government is forcibly converting Jews, one must die rather than violate even a minor practice . . . what is a minor practice? Even to change a shoelace (Sanhedrin 74a-b).*

Rashi explains that if the Jews wear their shoelaces tied in one style and the non-Jews wear them tied in a different style, it would be forbidden to change the way we do it if it was part of a forced conversion. Even though this is a custom and not a law, it is part of the Jewish identity and one may not alter it as a means of "passing." (Tosfos explain that the Jews wore black laces and the non-Jews wore white laces, but the principle is the same for color as for style.)

We Don't Care What Society Does

> *Do not act like they do in Egypt where you used to live, nor like they do in Canaan where I am bringing you. Do not follow their practices (Vayikra 18:3).*

This is a specific commandment not to copy the practices of the nations where we live. Just because everyone around us dresses or acts in a certain fashion doesn't make it acceptable.

Not to Copy Other Nations' Ways

> *They did not destroy the nations which Hashem commanded them to. Instead, they mingled with them and learned their ways. They served their idols and (the nations) became a trap for them (Tehillim 106:34-36).*

Mingling with the other nations and copying their ways was a trap for the Jews in the time of Yehoshua (Joshua). It ultimately led to them turning away from Hashem.

Who Wears the Pants in Your Family?

Even though I do not intend to provide a definitive list of "permitted" and "prohibited" garments, I do wish to examine the *halachic* process as it pertains to at least one *tzniyus* issue. I have chosen the topic of pants (alluded to in the previous chapter) for a number of reasons. First of all, it's presumably a topic of relevance. If I were writing for a Bais Yaakov audience, it would be a foregone conclusion that women don't wear pants. Second of all, it's a "big" issue. There may be reasons why some communities wear tights and others wear socks or why these girls wear their sleeves to their elbows and those wear sleeves to their wrists, but those differences are not as obvious to the casual observer as the fact that some girls wear pants and others wear only skirts.

There are a number of *tzniyus* issues which people mistakenly think have no real history behind them. These include issues such as women wearing pants and the height of *mechitzas*. The reason people think that these are strictly modern issues is because there was not a lot written about them until recent years. This is wrong. The reason there was not a lot written about these issues is because they were not challenged. Nobody asked a Rav in the fourteenth century about women wearing pants because, religious issues aside, women just weren't wearing pants.

One reference to the practice of women wearing skirts can be traced to the *pasuk* (verse) in *Shir HaShirim* 7:2, "*How beautiful are your footsteps in your shoes, Princess. Your thighs are hidden, they are like jewels, the work of a craftsman's hands.*[1]" The praise refers to the shape of a woman's thighs being concealed, not just covered. Sleeves *cover* the arms, but a skirt *conceals* the shape of a woman's legs. This and similar sources refer to the concept of *pisuk raglayim* (the split between the legs). According to this principle, a woman's thighs must be concealed. (The thighbone extends to behind the knee. This is why the knee is typically cited as the length a skirt must cover.)

There are several potential *halachic* problems with women wearing pants. The first is the above issue of *pisuk raglayim*. Another is the commandment of *lo yilbash*, that a man may not wear a woman's clothes and vice versa (*Devarim* 22:5). (Once women started wearing slacks, were they still considered a uniquely male garment? Read on!) The third problem is the issue of *b'chukoseihem lo seileichu*, that we may not adopt practices of the nations among whom we live (*Vayikra* 18:3). (For more on *b'chukoseihem*, skip back to our discussion on body piercing in the chapter on "Community Standards.")

The issue of *lo yilbash*—not to wear garments designated as appropriate attire for the opposite sex—was discussed in an article by Rabbi David Friedman in the *Journal of Halacha and Contemporary Society*, Number IV (1982). I contacted Rabbi Friedman, an old mentor and friend, and requested permission to summarize his research for the purpose of this chapter. He graciously agreed.

This next part gets a little technical and it may not be for everyone. I have provided a summary of the quoted opinions following the text in a fashion that some may prefer. (Those who wish can skip the section between the two rows of asterisks and go straight to the bullet points.)

* * *

In the Gemara (*Nazir* 49), the *Tanna Kama* (first opinion) says that *lo yilbash* means that men and women should not dress up and try to pass as the opposite gender. Rabbi Eliezer ben Yaakov expresses the opinion that it means that a woman should not use men's instruments such as weapons, while men should not wear women's articles such as jewelry. The question is whether Rabbi Eliezer completely disagrees with the *Tanna Kama* or whether he is adding to the first opinion. The *Smag* (*Lav* 60) says that Rabbi Eliezer is adding to the *Tanna Kama*'s opinion because a verse from the Torah never departs from its literal meaning.

The *Bach* (*Yoreh Deah* 182) further explains the *Smag*. Rabbi Eliezer defines "clothes" as objects of beauty and adornment which might be worn by members of the opposite sex for immoral purposes. The *Smag* tells us that even utilitarian items may not be worn for the purposes of immorality. But if there is no intent for promiscuity, it would be permitted.

The *Bach* and the *Taz* (*Yoreh Deah* 182:4) express another lenient opinion, that one may wear objects designated for the other gender as protection from the elements.

The Rambam (*Hilchos Avodah Zarah* 12:10) rules like Rabbi Eliezer, although he does not qualify it by ascribing it to the intention of the wearer. According to the Rambam, wearing clothes of the other gender would be prohibited regardless of the intent. He abolished a local custom of a bride dancing with a helmet and sword on the basis that it violated a Torah prohibition, even though the intent was clearly entertainment and not immorality. The *Sefer HaChinuch* (*Mitzvos* 542-543) also does not consider intent a factor.

The *Shulchan Aruch* (*Yoreh Deah* 182:4) quotes the Rambam and would appear to agree that intent doesn't matter. The *Ramah* (*Orach Chaim* 696:8) defends the practice of men dressing in women's clothes on Purim for entertainment purposes, but various authorities including the *Shach* (182:4) and the *Mishna Brura* (696:30) disagree with the *Ramah* (and therefore the *Bach*).

By this point we have a difference of opinion regarding whether or not intention makes a difference in wearing garments designated for the opposite sex. Those of the opinion that intent makes no difference appear to be in the majority and to get the last word. But now the question is: are pants a garment designated for men?

In large part this hinges on whether the status of a garment can change as society's practice changes. If a garment was once worn by only one gender and is now worn by both genders, does that change its *halachic* status?

The Rashba (*Shailos & Teshuvos* 4, 90) says that if someone starts doing something prohibited, even if he convinces many others to follow his example, it does not change the act into a permitted one. This opinion of the Rashba was used by Rabbi Yitzchak Yaakov Weiss to support his opinion that pants are still essentially a male garment, despite societal acceptance to the contrary (*Minchas Yitzchak* II, 108). Rabbi Eliezer Wohldenberg suggested that the leniency of the *Bach* could only be employed in a manner that was still clearly feminine, such as wearing pants with a skirt over it. He goes on to state that no *halachic* authority ever considered the style of dress in rendering a decision unless the reason for the style was functional (*Tzitz Eliezer* XI, 62).

A lenient opinion regarding *lo yilbash* is proposed by Rav Ovadiah Yosef, who says that garments now commonly worn by both genders would not violate the prohibition of *lo yilbash*. But even Rav Ovadiah Yosef does not permit women to wear pants based on issues of *tzniyus* and *b'chukoseihem lo seileichu* (not following secular practices).

We see that there is no universal consensus regarding whether pants violate the prohibition of *lo yilbash*. Rabbi Friedman concludes his article by saying that the various authorities would agree that wearing pants is prohibited because of the *tzniyus* issues (discussed at the beginning of this chapter) and that the relevance of *lo yilbash* would be in a case where modesty was not an issue, such as under a skirt while skiing, skating or climbing.

* * *

Okay, that ends the technical stuff. Let's review the opinions:

- The *Tanna Kama* of the Gemara: men and women may not wear garments unique to the other gender in an attempt to pass as the opposite gender.
- Rabbi Eliezer ben Yaakov: men and women may not even use the other gender's accessories.
- The *Smag*: Rabbi Eliezer is adding to the *Tanna Kama*'s opinion, rather than disagreeing with it.
- The *Bach*: if there is no intent for promiscuity, opposite gender garments would be permitted.
- The *Bach* and the *Taz*: one may wear garments of the other gender as protection from the elements.
- The Rambam and The *Sefer HaChinuch*: men and women may not wear the others' garments regardless of the intention of the wearer.
- The Shulchan Aruch: appears to agree that intent doesn't matter.
- The Ramah: allows men to wear women's clothes on Purim for entertainment.
- The *Mishna Brura* and the *Shach* disagree with the *Ramah* and the *Bach*.
- Rabbi Yitzchak Yaakov Weiss: pants are still a male garment, despite societal acceptance.
- Rabbi Eliezer Wohldenberg: the leniency of the *Bach* could only be employed in a feminine manner, such as with a skirt over it.

- Rav Ovadiah Yosef: garments now commonly worn by both genders do not violate *lo yilbash*, but there are still issues of *tzniyus* and *b'chukoseihem lo seileichu*.

My purpose in summarizing this *halachic* debate is to demonstrate that the rules and accepted practices of *tzniyus* are not arbitrary. They are part of a process that starts with the Torah, wends its way through the Talmud, down through the *Rishonim* (early commentators), *Acharonim* (later commentators) and to the modern *poskim* (*halachic* decisors). This discussion is only about one aspect (*lo yilbash*) pertaining to one issue (pants). And in that one issue, there are still the aspects of *pisuk raglayim* and *b'chukoseihem*, which we have not analyzed. Now you have the start of an idea of what Torah authorities must evaluate when considering issues such as whether women may wear pants.

Working in Jewish education, I receive a lot of questions on this particular topic. The most common question I get in this area is: Which is better—to wear a short, tight skirt or loose baggy pants? I must have been asked this question one-hundred times. Only once was it actually asked in the context of a real-life issue. The other ninety-nine times it was a hypothetical scenario.

The response I gave the 99 times is, "Which is better? To eat a ham sandwich or a cheeseburger?" They're both *treif* (non-kosher)! Even though the meat of the cheeseburger may be beef, it wasn't slaughtered according to the laws of *kashrus*, it wasn't soaked and salted, and adding the cheese makes it even worse! The correct answer is not to eat either; go get a kosher hamburger instead!

The same thing is true with the "forced choice" of a short, tight skirt or baggy pants. They both have problems. Why worry about which has fewer problems when there's a "kosher" option available, namely appropriate skirts?

What about the one-out-of-a-hundred who had a real-life scenario? (The context of the question was an issue with a choice of school uniforms.) This happens to be the very same as a well-known question that Rav Ovadiah Yosef answered. People mistakenly believe that Rav Ovadiah Yosef generally permits women to wear pants. He actually permitted it in one specific circumstance where there was a "forced choice" between slacks or even more inappropriate skirts. He chose pants as the lesser of the evils in this particular situation. Should you ever have this it as a real-life issue, ask a Rabbi what the lesser evil would be in your case.

Another question I received came from a girl who started off by telling me that she had worn only skirts for two years. She proceeded to tell me that she was going to Israel for the summer and that she would be doing a lot of hiking and climbing there. She wanted to know whether it would be permitted to wear pants for those activities. I told her that there might be people who would permit that, but I asked whether it was really what she wanted. A trip to Israel, I told her, should be spiritually elevating. I asked whether wearing pants for the first time in two years was something that would make her feel elevated. Even if she found someone who permitted it, spiritually it's a step backwards from the progress she had made. Instead, I advised her to wear pants under a loose flared skirt for these activities (as in the conclusion of Rabbi Friedman's article, above).

Despite the advice to wear pants under a skirt for activities which might be immodest, this might not be advisable for everyday wear. When I was in high school, girls would occasionally return to class after gym wearing their sweatpants or jeans under their skirts. If they were caught by the principal, he would send them to the bathroom to remove the pants, which he would then confiscate. At the time I couldn't understand why this was problematic; wasn't a skirt and pants *twice* as modest?

Now I understand it better. I have seen girls at *Shabbatonim* who wear the skirt/pants combo on Saturday night or in the small hours of the morning. And you know what? A lot of them act as if they're wearing pants. The way they sit and climb and act in general is not the way they would if they were wearing skirts only. It's less refined. Less ladylike. They would never sit or act that way in skirts alone.

So now we have discussed some issues regarding pants. Hopefully this gives one an idea of the issues surrounding this mode of dress, as well as how we reach the accepted practice.

Selected Torah Sources pertaining to Women Wearing Pants

Skirts

> *Her impurity was evident from the hems of her garments, she gave no thought to her end . . . (Eicha 1:9).*

Watch the length and the slits, ladies!

> *How beautiful are your footsteps in your shoes, Princess. Your thighs are hidden, they are like jewels, the work of a craftsman's hands (Shir HaShirim 7:2).*

The praise refers to the shape of a woman's thighs being concealed, not just covered. (See footnote 1, below.) From here we infer the propriety of skirts for women. The modest traits in this verse are compared to jewels which have been carefully polished by expert jewelers. Similarly, these habits are carefully honed by Jewish girls.

(As far as the first part of the verse, which praises the footsteps of the Jewish girls, contrast with *Yeshaya* 3:16, "the girls of Israel have become full of themselves . . . walking with deliberate steps.")

> *The school of Rabbi Yishmael taught: what did the Mishkan (Tabernacle) resemble? It looked like a woman walking in the marketplace, with the skirts trailing behind (Shabbos 98b).*

This statement is used by the *Gemara* to conjure an image of how the curtains of the *Mishkan* trailed behind. It is evident from this statement that women in the time of the *Gemara* typically wore long skirts or it would not have been an effective simile. (How nice and appropriate it is that the *Mishkan*, the place where Hashem's presence dwelled, is compared to a woman!)

Transvestism

> *A man's article shall not be on a woman, nor shall a man wear a woman's clothes because anyone who does this is an abomination to Hashem your God (Devarim 22:5).*

This clearly includes clothes, although some authorities extend the broader word *kli* (used to refer to a man's articles) to include religious articles (e.g., *tallis* and *tefillin*).

1. My translation of this verse is not what one would find in most English versions, which typically render it, "your rounded thighs" or some similar turn of a phrase. The meaning of the *pasuk* hinges on the word *chamukei*. In some contexts, the Hebrew word ChMK means to conceal or to hide away as in *Shir HaShirim* 5:6, "I opened the door for my lover, but he had disappeared (*chamak*)" The Gemara in *Moed Katan* 16a (last line) takes it as a given that *chamukei* in our verse means concealed. They cite the verse and continue by saying, "just as the thigh is concealed . . ." (See also Rashi there.)

   Verses in Tanach often lend themselves to alternate meanings. Does *Devarim* 26:5 mean "my ancestor was a wandering Aramenean" (as per the Sforno and others) or "an Aramenean tried to destroy my ancestor" (as rendered by Rashi, *et al*)? Does *Bereishis* 4:15 mean that Cain would be punished after seven generations or that if anyone killed Cain they would be punished sevenfold? This reality of multiple layers of meaning is particularly true in the case of *Shir HaShirim*, which is a profound allegory with surface meaning and many layers of subtext.

Sing, Sing a Song

(The title of this chapter works best if you sing it to the tune of the old Carpenters song, which younger readers may remember from *Sesame Street*.)

So what's all this business about *kol isha*, anyway?

Some people feel that the fact that women cannot sing in front of men is outdated, sexist, or just plain wrong.

I think these people are blind to the power of song.

When a woman sings, it can be a very emotional moment. Even if she doesn't dress like Madonna, Britney, J. Lo or (insert name of flavor of the month here).

When a woman sings, she bares a part of her soul. It can be a spiritual act. It can be a very personal moment. Maybe it *should* be private.

We have plenty of textual support for the practice of *kol isha*, but if we honestly examine the power of song, we might not even need it.

The first source is an example from the Torah itself, *Shemos* 15:20: "And Miriam the prophetess, the sister of Aaron, took a tambourine in her hand and all the women went out after her with tambourines and drums." We see that when *B'nei Yisroel* sang the Shira, the song of praise to Hashem at the Red Sea, the women went off to sing and dance separately from the men. We also see that the women used instruments, a detail not mentioned in the case of the men. Some commentators explain that the instruments helped to drown out the sound of their singing.

Our next source is from *Shir HaShirim* 2:15. In this verse, Shlomo HaMelech (King Solomon) writes, "Show me your face and let me hear your voice, because your voice is sweet and your appearance is attractive." The Gemara in *Brachos* (24a) uses this verse as the source for including a woman's voice when discussing the different parts of a woman which should be considered private and in whose presence *Shema* may not be said. Later Rabbis clarify that this refers specifically to singing rather than speaking.

The Gemara in *Megilla* is another source for much of our understanding of *kol isha*. The Mishna tells us that two people may read *Megillas Esther* simultaneously on Purim and that it still fulfills the listeners' obligation. Rashi explains that we are not concerned that two voices cannot be heard together. This appears to contradict the ruling in the case of reading the Torah and the Haftarah, that two voices reading together cannot be discerned. The Gemara explains that people pay extra attention to the reading of the *megilla* because it is of special interest to them. So we see that two voices would normally mix, but if one pays special attention, it is possible to single them out. (Presumably we would not consider three or more voices as individually discernible, even if we pay special attention.)

The Gemara in *Sotah* (39b), especially Tosfos there ("*Ad*"), discuss additional issues, such as whether the two voices are saying (or singing) the same thing or different things. Apparently, if one is saying or singing something, then one cannot simultaneously be listening to what someone else is saying or singing.

The current practice that many rely upon is based upon the belief that if three girls sing together, then it is no longer *kol isha*. But is this so? Let us see.

People often cite the famous *teshuva* (responsum) of Rav Yechiel Yaakov Weinberg in his *sefer, Seridei Aish*. The problem is that people remember one little piece of that *teshuva* and forget the details.

The context of the *teshuva* is that a school inquired as to the permissibility of their practice of boys and girls singing *Shabbos zemiros* and other songs together. The practice, which had been initiated with the endorsement of great German rabbis, was being opposed.

The *Seridei Aish* takes a number of things into consideration when evaluating this issue:

- The German rabbis were experts in educational methodology and were much more successful in stemming the tide of assimilation than their more traditional counterparts in Poland and Lithuania.
- The opposing rabbis, while well-versed in the *halacha*, were unaware of the extenuating circumstances in the geographic area under discussion.

- The Gemara discusses *kol isha* in the context of *ervah* (private parts) in whose presence *kriyat Shema* may not be recited. There are different opinions among the Rabbis regarding the permissibility of hearing a single girl (as opposed to a married woman) sing when it is not interfering with reciting *Shema*. (We rule that it makes no difference, but there is a dissenting opinion.)
- There is an opinion that *kol isha* may be prohibited only when it is listened to with romantic intent. Again, this is not how we rule, but there is such an opinion.[1]
- If *zemiros* or songs whose lyrics are verses from the Torah are being sung, that is intended to stir religious passion rather than romantic passion.

There are other factors discussed by Rav Weinberg in this *teshuva*[2], but these are some of the main points.

The thing that people have a tendency to overlook when citing this responsum is the context of the *shaila* (the question posed), i.e. the coed singing of *zemiros* and other holy songs for *kiruv* purposes. These details make a huge difference and ignoring the context or applying the leniency too broadly can present *halachic* problems. For example:

(1) Coed singing is not exclusively female; an all female choir of even 100 women may still be *kol isha*. (See the Gemara in *Sotah* 48a, quoted at the end of this chapter.)
(2) *Zemiros* and other Jewish songs would arguably stir religious feelings, as discussed above. This *heter* (leniency) would not work for rock and roll or Broadway show tunes.
(3) It must be for *kiruv* purposes. Even the *Seridei Aish* says that without this "it would be forbidden for young men to sing Shabbos *zemiros* with young women."

It is important for people to rely upon *heterim* (leniencies) only in their appropriate contexts.[3] For example, it's not a violation of *tzniyus* for a girl to be examined by her doctor, but that doesn't mean that he can undress her in a non-medical context on the basis that he's "seen it already." Similarly, there are times when a girl may be permitted to sing with men. But that doesn't mean that it is appropriate in *every* situation.

Here's another *kol isha* issue: Many men who would never attend a concert or a play in which women sing have no problem listening to women sing on a tape or in a movie.[4] That's because a tape of a voice is not a voice. (The Gemara in *Sanhedrin* 45a says that the *yetzer hara*—the desire for the forbidden—only drives a person towards that which he can see. A woman's voice in the absence of the woman herself is therefore permissible according to some.) If you heard someone say a *bracha* on a tape, you would not respond "Amen." (Well, maybe you would, but if you did, you'd be wrong.) You could not fulfill a *mitzvah* such as hearing the *megilla* or the *shofar* through a tape recording, so arguably one could not violate a rule such as *kol isha*, either. (Again, this is one opinion, not a universally accepted constant.)

This is not inconsistent with the reality that looking at pictures of inappropriately dressed women is not allowed. The fact that a woman's breasts, thighs, hair (if married) and voice are all classified as "private" doesn't mean that the details of their privacy are all identical. I'll provide you with several examples using hair to illustrate the concept:

- Other body parts become an *ervah* (private part) as soon as a girl reaches a certain age. Not even delayed physical development would keep a twelve-year-old girl from being required to cover certain parts of herself. But hair only becomes an *ervah* if the woman is married. Take two 25-year-olds, even twin sisters; if one is married, her hair is considered private and the other woman's isn't.
- If a girl goes mixed swimming, she may have her picture taken at the beach. If she later starts acting in a more *tzniyus* fashion and avoids mixed swimming, she would probably take those pictures and put them away where they could not be seen by boys, even those with whom she had once been swimming. But most women who start covering their hair after marriage would probably not hide all of their pre-marriage photographs in which their hair was uncovered.[5]
- Few Rabbinic authorities would criticize a woman for covering her hair with a *sheitel* (wig), so long as it is not so lifelike that it could easily be mistaken for her own hair; in fact, in many communities it would be expected. But if she wore a long-sleeved T-shirt that had a picture of a bikini top drawn on the chest, even if it were clearly a cartoon, people would recognize it as grossly immodest, even though she is completely covered. Covering hair with something that looks like hair is not a problem; covering the chest with something that is suggestive of breasts would be a problem.

From these examples it is obvious that there are different levels of *ervah*. Voice is clearly in a category different from that of skin.

First of all, our own experience tells us that there is a practical difference between a man listening to a woman speaking and singing. This is not the case with other types of *ervah*. It is immodest for a man to watch a woman breast-feed an infant; he cannot justify it because it's "functional." If a part is private, it is always private (excepting situations such as a doctor with a patient, of course). But a man can listen to a woman's voice in certain contexts (speech) and not in others (song).

Consider this: it would be grossly immodest for a man to view a woman in a state of undress. To see several women undressed together would be considerably even more inappropriate. To see a large group of men and women all undressed together would be off the immodesty scale altogether and would be in the realm of overt immorality. But while a man may not listen to a woman or several women sing, he could possibly listen to a large group of men and women singing together (as in the *teshuva* of the *Seridei Aish*). While increasing the number of participants and mixing the group would make the case of viewing nudity even more problematic, it alleviates some of the issues of *kol isha*. We see from these examples that while the voice is still a potentially private part of a woman, it is obviously not identical in practice to the rules regarding flesh.

That last statement works the other way, as well. Even though *kol isha* may not be identical in practice to the rules regarding the exposure of flesh, the voice is still a very stirring, a very powerful, and potentially a very private part of a woman.

1. The *S'dei Chemed* is occasionally cited as an authority lenient in this regard, but in actuality, he acknowledges this position while recommending against it.
2. Not the least of which is the halachic principle of *"eis laasos laShem,"* a rarely-utilized power of the Rabbis, based on *Tehillim* 119:126 and described in *Temurah* 14. Rav Weinberg ruled that it was preferable to be lenient in this case than to let a generation assimilate, though he was quick to point out in no uncertain terms that only the leading rabbinic authorities of a generation

can decide what constitutes "*eis laasos laShem*" and that individuals may *not* make this kind of call for themselves.)
3. Refer to the *teshuva* of Rav Ovadiah Yosef discussed in the footnotes of the chapter "Community Standards."
4. Of course, many men would not listen to women sing on a tape and many women would object to men listening to them on tape. Even a man who does listen to taped women singing should not listen to the taped songs of a woman he knows. The Gemara in *Avodah Zara* (20b) says that a man may not stare at clothes belonging to a woman he knows because he will come to fantasize about her wearing it. Just as he can associate her clothes with her person (in her absence), he can associate her singing voice with her person. Associating the recorded voice with a woman he knows, as opposed to a woman he does not know, could lead to *hirhurim* (inappropriate thoughts or fantasies), which are to be avoided.
5. On the other hand, some would. This is a praiseworthy sensitivity to *tzniyus*, but it does not appear to be inherently required.

Selected Torah Sources Regarding Kol Isha

The Voice

> *My dove in the clefts of the rocks, in the hidden parts of the cliff, show me your face and let me hear your voice, because your voice is sweet and your appearance is attractive (Shir HaShirim 2:15).*

This verse compares one's voice to one's appearance. Just as there is modesty in dress there is modesty in speech and song.

> *Shmuel says a woman's voice is sexual based upon the verse "your voice is sweet and your appearance is attractive" (Brachos 24a).*

Separate Dancing

> *And Miriam the prophetess, the sister of Aaron, took a tambourine in her hand and all the women went out after her with tambourines and drums (Shemos 15:20).*

We see from this that the women did not dance with the men and that they separated some distance so that they could sing in private.

Kol Isha

> *Rav Yosef said, "when men sing and women respond to it, that's promiscuous behavior. When women sing and men respond to it, that's playing with fire." What's the practical difference (if both are bad)? You have to clamp down on the (case of women singing before men) more harshly than on (the case of men singing in front of women) (Sotah 48a).*

Rav Yosef is of the opinion that women might find it attractive when men sing, but it's nothing compared to the attraction men feel when women sing.

In the Shul:
SheLo Asani Isha and Mechitza

While there are many differences between men and women in the synagogue, few seem to burn women up as badly as the *bracha* men say, "*shelo asani isha*" ("that God did not create me a woman") and *mechitzas*, which separate the genders.

The fact that females do not count as part of the *minyan* or put on *Tefillin* are more readily accepted by women in the Orthodox community than these two issues. Rather than just rely on "men and women have different spiritual needs" (as discussed earlier, in "The Difference"), I believe that these two items require a little further elaboration.

A. The Bracha of SheLo Asani Isha

The *bracha* of *shelo asani isha* is part of a triumvirate of similar *brachos* including *shelo asani goy* ("that God did not create me a non-Jew") and *shelo asani aved* ("that God did not create me a slave"). Think about these two *brachos*. Not wanting to be a slave is pretty self-evident, right? It's hard work. You get whipped. Nobody in their right mind would want to be a slave.

Actually, the Torah's brand of slavery is not at all like the slavery we experienced in Egypt or that which African-Americans experienced in the South. Torah slavery is more like a job that comes with room and board. Slaves had rights. Their masters could not abuse them. They could not mistreat them. If there was only one pillow in the house, the master had to give it to the slave. Slavery even had an expiration date. A slave might find his situation so desirable that he would refuse to leave when his term of service was up! (See *Shemos* 21:5.) So, clearly, the meaning of *shelo asani aved* is not what we first thought.[1]

Similarly, the intent of *shelo asani goy* is also not mean-spirited. (The word "*goy*" literally means nation; it's *not* a racial slur. However, since non-Jews do take offense at it, it is not polite to use it out of a proper Hebrew context.) Which do you think is easier, being Jewish or Protestant? In case you have any doubts, let me ask you a few more questions. How many children lament the absence of a Christmas tree in their lives? How many parents justify the addition of a "Hannukah bush" to fill that imagined void? Why are intermarriage and assimilation such vital issues in the Jewish community? It's clearly because, like the old Yiddish saying goes, *es iz shver tzu zain a yid* (it's hard to be a Jew). Since so many Jews wish they were born WASPs, why do the rest of us thank God for the hard life?

The answer to all of these issues is the same. We thank Hashem for the opportunity to do *mitzvos*. A non-Jew has seven *mitzvos* he must fulfill, the *Sheva Mitzvos B'nei Noach* (seven commandments for the descendants of Noah, i.e. every human being on the planet). These are all of the fairly obvious kind: not to kill, not to steal, not to curse Hashem, to establish courts of justice, etc. Jews have 613 *mitzvos*. Harder? Sure. But we thank Hashem for the greater opportunity to serve Him.

Jewish slaves have obligations, too. But because of their obligations to their masters, the Torah limits their religious requirements. A slave is exempt from *mitzvos asei she'hazman grama*, positive *mitzvos* which are only performed at specific times. Jewish slavery may be a relatively cushy and secure position, but we would rather have the greater obligation in *mitzvos*.

As we already discussed, women are also exempt from *mitzvos asei she'hazman grama*. The reason behind the *bracha* of *shelo asani isha* is therefore for men to thank Hashem for the opportunity to serve Him by doing more *mitzvos*. It is not to thank Him for making us masters of the world, or for sparing us from the pain of childbirth and menstrual cramps, or for any other explanation the secular world may ascribe to it. Like the *brachos* of *shelo asani goy* and *shelo asani aved*, it has one purpose and one purpose only, and that purpose is not intended to disparage anyone who was born into any of the "*shelo asani*" categories.

Women also have their own *bracha*. They say "*she'asani kirtzono*" ("that Hashem created me according to His will"). The secular world likes to paint that *bracha* as sort of a "consolation prize." "Well, I may only be a woman," they imagine thousands of Jewish girls *davening* every morning, "but at least I'm the way God wants me." That's not even close.

Arguably, *she'asani kirtzono* is the "better" *bracha* of the two. First of all, it's phrased in the positive. Since when do we thank Hashem for acts He didn't do? Think about other *brachos*, aside from the three *shelo asanis*. You'd be hard pressed to find another *bracha* phrased in the negative. We generally thank Hashem for things He did (and does), not for things He didn't (or doesn't) do. Since positive *brachos* are the norm, the question is not why women say *she'asani kirtzono*, but rather why men don't.

Because they can't.

Men weren't created according to Hashem's will.

Hashem wants Jewish males to be circumcised. They aren't made that way. They have to be "fixed" on the eighth day by performing the *bris milah*. We can't say "God made me the way He wants me to be" because He didn't.

As a side comment, everything God made in the six days of creation was made in ascending order. Fish came after plants. Mammals came after birds. Man came after all the animals. So what came after man?

Woman.

Chava (Eve) was created after Adam. If Creation reflects an increasing spiritual order, then woman is the pinnacle of creation.

Disparage women through our *brachos*? *Chas v'shalom*! (God forbid!) The difference in the *brachos* recited by women and men each day simply reflects their unique spiritual gifts.

B. Mechitza

There are many different types and styles of *mechitzos* (partitions) used by *shuls* to separate the men from the women. There are short *mechitzos* and tall *mechitzos*, translucent *mechitzos* and opaque *mechitzos*. There are women's sections behind the men's section, next to the men's section and on balconies that overlook the men's section. I saw one *mechitza* in Baltimore that was a large screen that worked like a two-way mirror; it was solid black on the men's side but like a huge clear window on the women's side. How can we account for such wide variations in style? And if some *mechitzos* are short, virtually transparent screens, why do other *shuls* insist on opaque partitions that reach high above everyone's heads?

Remember when we discussed community standards? Well, there are a number of different opinions regarding the exact role that a *mechitza* is supposed to play. The size and style of a *mechitza* reflect in large part the purpose the *mechitza* is perceived to accomplish.

Before we discuss the different perceptions regarding the purpose of *mechitza*, let us first discuss the origins of the practice.

A Biblical source for the concept of segregating the genders at certain times is found in *Zechariah* 12:12 which refers to men mourning in one group and women mourning in another group. The *Gemara* in *Sukkah* (51a-b) discusses a problem of frivolity in the *Beis HaMikdash*. It uses this verse from *Zechariah* to determine that if the genders separate at a time of mourning when frivolous behavior is not likely to occur, then they should certainly separate at a time when inappropriate behavior such as flirting is likely. (If you don't think *shul* is a place where frivolity and flirting are likely to occur, you haven't seen the fashion shows some places put on!)

Now that we have seen the sources indicating that a *mechitza* is necessary, we must ask why there are such divergent practices. Almost all accepted opinions spring from two divergent statements of the Rambam, one in his *Peirush HaMishnayos* (Commentary on the Mishna), the other from the *Yad Chazakah* (also known as the *Mishneh Torah*). In one place, the Rambam writes that a *mechitza* was erected at the *Simchas Beis HaShoeva*, the festive water-drawing ceremony in the *Beis HaMikdash*, to prevent the men and women from *mingling*. In the other he states that it was done so that they should not *see one another*.

So which is it? If a *mechitza* exists so that men and women don't mix, a simple string might do the trick. If it exists so they don't see one another, we might need a wall. Is it even enough for men not to see the women? Maybe it means that both genders shouldn't see the other at all!

The different opinions come from the ways in which different authorities interpret and reconcile the differences in language used by the Rambam. Is one statement clarifying the other? Did the Rambam change his mind?

While all authorities agree to the necessity of the mechitza, and to a certain minimum standard, there are a wide variety of practices embraced by different communities. These accepted variations, as with other *minhagim* (community customs), all have Torah authorities who support them, as is necessary.

There is some leeway when it comes to *mechitza* height. What is minimally acceptable may not be what is optimal. And individual circumstances may lead to occasional leniencies. Rabbi Moshe Feinstein *ztz"l*, for example, wrote in *Igros Moshe* that the proper height for a *mechitza* is shoulder height (18 handbreaths, which is about five feet). On the one hand, he said that wherever possible it was preferable to have the *mechitza* be taller than this minimum acceptable height. On the other hand, Rav Moshe did permit lower *mechitzas* in some communities where he felt women would not attend *shul* at all if they couldn't see what was going on.

The fact that R. Moshe permitted lower *mechitzas* in some individual circumstances doesn't mean that every *shul* can automatically rely on that *heter* (exemption). Exceptions in such situations are made by recognized authorities on a case by case basis predicated upon individual circumstances. In this sense a *posek* (authority in Jewish law) is like a doctor. If you and I each have a bad cough, it doesn't mean I should automatically take your prescription medication. You might have a bacterial infection, while mine might be viral. Similar symptoms do not automatically mean the same cause or that we require the same treatment.

Heterim for low *mechitzas* were not meant to be unnecessarily embraced by shuls without compelling reasons; just the opposite, in fact! R. Moshe suggested *exceeding* the minimally acceptable height wherever possible. If a Torah giant such as Rav Moshe gave us advice meant to enhance the sanctity of our synagogues, we should not dismiss it out of hand. These leniencies should only be pursued when circumstances truly warrant them, and even then, they must be decided only by qualified *halachic* authorities.

The bottom line is that a *mechitza* is like a hemline. There are reasons why different communities accept different standards. But all legitimate communal standards are determined by the Torah authorities of those communities, in conformity with parameters set by recognized Torah authorities.

1. There is a difference between an *eved K'naani* (Canaanite slave) and an *eved Ivri* (Hebrew slave). The latter were the kind who were essentially hired help for an extended period, but even the former had more rights than we generally associate with slaves.

Selected Torah Sources on Separating the Genders

Mechitza

> *Originally the women sat inside and the men sat outside (in the Beis HaMikdash), but as this led to levity, it was changed so that the women sat outside and the men sat inside. Since that still led to levity, it was changed again so that the women sat in an upper gallery and the men sat below (Sukkah 51b).*

Yichud

> *Rav Kahana said, if there are men in the outer room and women in the inner room, we are not afraid of yichud (i.e. that an unmarried man and woman will become secluded together), but if men are in the inner room and women are in the outer room, we are. A braisa (a teaching contemporary with the Mishna) taught it the other way around. Abaye said that since Rav Kahana taught it one way and the braisa taught it the other, we should be careful about both circumstances. Accordingly, Abaye made a partition out of barrels. Rava made a partition out of reeds (Kiddushin 81a).*

Rashi explains Rav Kahana's reason as follows: if the men are in the inner room, they must pass through the outer room to exit, but if the men are in the outer room, they have no reason to enter the inner room. The opinion of the *braisa* is that if men are in the outer room, one of them can slip into the inner room undetected. Since logical reasons were given as to why *yichud* could happen in either case, Abaye and Rava set up *mechitzas* (partitions) at lectures, weddings and other places where men and women gathered.

Segregation of the Sexes

> *Young men and also maidens, the elderly with the young, let them praise the name of God . . . (Tehillim 148:12-13).*

Why does this verse say the young "with" the old, but boys "and also" girls? While there's no reason for the different ages not to praise Hashem together, it's appropriate for the sexes to participate separately, even in this lofty activity.

The Myth of "Shomer Negiah"

Don't read the title of this chapter and get your hopes up. Don't break out the slow-dance music just yet. The myth isn't what you think I mean. (At least it's not what many readers are going to *hope* I mean.)

First, let's define some terms. "*Shomer*" comes from the verb *lishmor*, meaning to guard or to watch. In context it means to observe a law. Someone who is "*shomer Shabbat*" is "Sabbath-observant." "*Negiah*" means touch. So to be "*shomer negiah*" ostensibly means to "observe the laws of touching." I do not believe that being "*shomer negiah*" is an authentic concept in Judaism, but, again, not for the reasons one might think (or hope).

Did you ever speak *lashon hara* (gossip) and have someone chastise you for it? (This normally takes place in the form of the listener shrieking "*Lashon hara!*" in as shrill a voice as possible.) There are three possible responses: the good, the bad and the unnatural.

- The good response would be to say, "Oops! You're right!" and then to stop speaking *lashon hara*.
- The bad response would be to say, "I don't care," and to continue speaking *lashon hara*.
- The unnatural response would be to say, "It's okay—I'm not *shomer lashon hara!*"

That's because, while *lashon hara* is a valid concept in Judaism, there is no concept of being "*shomer*" it.[1]

Similarly, nobody says "I keep Pesach and Sukkos, but I'm not *shomer* Shavuos." If somebody doesn't check their clothes for *shaatnez*, the forbidden mixture of wool and linen, they never say it's because they're "not *shomer shaatnez*."

73

But when it comes to "*negiah*" (I'll tell you in a minute why I put that word in quotes), for some reason people say, "It's okay—I'm not *shomer negiah*." (Actually, they don't even use the full term "*shomer negiah*" anymore; they just say "*shomer*" because everybody knows what they mean.)

I'll tell you why people use the term "*shomer negiah*." Because "*negiah*" is fun. By saying "*shomer negiah*," people create the illusion that this law is somehow optional. If it's optional, one doesn't have to feel obligated to keep it or to feel bad if one doesn't. Sephardic Jews, for example, don't feel apologetic about eating *kitniyos* (legumes) on Pesach because refraining from *kitniyos* is an Ashkenazic, not a Sephardic practice. So people use the term "*shomer negiah*" in a misguided attempt to delude themselves into thinking that they can "opt out" of following the laws of interpersonal behavior.

(The reason I put "*negiah*" in quotes is because, while that is the term that is used colloquially, it is not how this concept is referred to in *halachic* literature. The proper term is "*kiruv basar*," "nearness of flesh.")

So let's talk about *negiah*. (To keep things simple, we'll continue to call it *negiah*, rather than *kiruv basar*, and we'll skip the quotes now that the point has been made.)

The source of this *halacha*, as stated in our sources chapter, is *Vayikra* 18:6 which states, "No person may draw close to any prohibited relationship in order to initiate sexual contact." The operative words are "draw close." We are not permitted to do those acts which are a prelude to sex, i.e. any intimate contact between a male person and a female person who are not married or closely related to one another.

This doesn't mean that there is no context in which a male and a female may touch. A male doctor touches his female patients. It doesn't even have to be life-threatening; a female dental hygienist touches her male patients. (Permitted forms of contact may not necessarily be medical in nature, though these examples happen to be. The farther we get from medical necessity, though, the more difference of opinion there will be.)

But what about friendly touches such as handshakes and "high fives?" Those could hardly be considered overtures to sex, so why are those prohibited forms of contact?

Because they are more intimate than we normally acknowledge.

I will once again bring an example from popular culture. I have never seen this concept demonstrated more clearly than by Quentin Tarantino in the movie *Pulp Fiction*. John Travolta and Samuel L. Jackson portray two hit men who, in one scene, discuss a colleague who was presumably thrown off a roof for giving the wife of a mob boss a foot massage. In discussing whether this is an overreaction, they question whether or not a foot massage is a sexual act.

"Of course it's not sexual," one maintained, "it's just feet."

"Let me ask you this," the other retorted, "would you let a *man* give you a foot massage?"

The only response the first character could make to an observation this obvious was, "Shut up."

Seemingly innocuous gestures such as a handshake may appear meaningless, but they actually have more power than we normally ascribe to them. When Israeli Prime Minister Yitzhak Rabin met Yasser Arafat at the White House, he shook his hand. The Jewish public and press lambasted him over it. Why did everyone go nuts if this was a "meaningless" gesture? If they were sitting down to dinner with the president, nobody would have yelled, "How could you pass the salt to that murderer?" Clearly there is more to a "mere" handshake than we normally consider.[2]

As powerful as same sex touch can be (and it is), inter-gender touch is exponentially more evocative (for most of the population). Even a seemingly innocuous friendly touch, such as a tap or a pat, contains an element that it lacks between members of the same sex. The friendlier the contact, the stronger the connection becomes. One of the most common things I hear is, "But, *Rabbi*," (there's always a whine there), "just because I hold his hand, it doesn't mean that I'm going to end up in bed with him!" True. It doesn't mean that at all. But everybody who *does* end up in bed together started out holding hands!

Here's another *pasuk* pertaining to *negiah*: the end of *parshas Acharei Mos* (*Vayikra* 18) deals with the *arayos*, forbidden sexual relationships. The next *parsha*, *Kedoshim*, begins with "Speak to the entire assembly of *B'nei Yisroel* and tell them 'You shall be holy because I, Hashem your God, am holy'" (*Vayikra* 19:2). Rashi quotes the *Midrash* in *Vayikra Rabbah* which explains that this refers specifically to the area of sexuality because every place the Torah discusses sex it also discusses being holy. (Several examples are given by Rashi.)

Our Sages also tell us that, since the Torah has just finished outlining the prohibited sexual acts, the admonition to be holy must refer to acts that are *permitted*. (Compare with *Yevamos* 20a, "sanctify yourself with that which is permissible to you.") Just because sex is permitted in certain contexts (i.e. marriage), that doesn't mean that people have *carte blanche* to do it all the time and in any manner they can conceive.

The perfect analogy for rules regarding things which are permitted is food. Food is obviously allowed, but there are limits. *Kashrus* is the most obvious; we are not permitted to eat pork or shellfish or meat-and-milk combinations. But even with kosher food there are rules. One has to make a *bracha*. One has to wash before bread and *bentch* after eating. Could one get up in the morning, wash, eat all day without making any additional *brachos*, and *bentch* before bed? Sure, if done within certain parameters it would be possible and it might not be a "sin," but that doesn't make it right. It is possible to be a *menuval birshus haTorah*[3], that is, a person who does things which are disgusting or reprehensible without violating any Torah laws. If one can do this with food, you bet it can be done with sex.

Judaism does not consider sex to be dirty or evil. It's good and natural, but it has to be kept to its proper context. *Chazal* have harsh words for scholars who are always after their wives "like roosters," that is, they do not have control over their passions. But the same Torah that prohibits indiscriminate sex also requires sex on certain occasions. The very first commandment in the Torah is to "be fruitful and multiply" (*Bereishis* 1:28). A man has to provide his wife with certain necessities, one of which is his conjugal duty to her. While the Torah permits a man to marry more than one woman (prohibited in most Jewish communities since a Rabbinic edict issued in the tenth century CE), he is not allowed to do so if it would reduce the amount of food, clothing or sexual interludes to which his existing wife has become accustomed (see *Shemos* 21:10). This not only encourages the act between man and wife, but it acknowledges the reality that women enjoy it as much as men do.

Judaism's outlook on sex is "all good things in moderation." The extreme philosophies of hedonism and asceticism are equally anathema to Judaism. (Hedonism is that idea that if it feels good, one should do it and that if it moves, it is okay to have sex with it. According to asceticism, sex is, at best, a necessary evil and that total abstinence is a lofty goal.)

It's natural for men and women to be attracted to one another. Regarding the creation of man, the Torah tells us that "male and female He created them" (*Bereishis* 1:27). The Midrash explains that man was originally one being comprising both genders. When God separated woman from man, they became two beings. It is quite natural for each gender, therefore, to seek its "missing piece." The Torah consequently says, "a man will therefore leave his father and mother and cling to his wife so that they will be like one person" (*Bereishis* 2:24). Please note that the Torah prescribes clinging to one's wife, not to every coed that looks good in a sweater, to the local barmaid or to a series of one night stands. Sex is encouraged and good *in its proper context.*

Now here's the problem. Love may be blind, but it's also a little stupid. We covered the whole men-and-women-are-different, Mars and Venus kind of stuff earlier in this book. Well, teenage boys and girls are very different, probably even more so than adult men and women. Both genders' hormones are out of control, the boys' typically about twenty times more than the girls'.

The problem is that boys and girls crave physical and emotional attention in different amounts. For simplicity's sake, we'll call emotional attention "love" and physical attention "sex," although it doesn't actually have to be "sex." Most girls crave "love" and are willing to give some amount of "sex" to receive it. Most boys crave "sex" and are willing to give what passes for "love" in hopes of receiving that. In the end, it's not a fair transaction.

For the most part, teenage hormones turn boys into animals and make girls a little stupid in this regard. It's not a criticism, it's a biological reality. Even very nice, sweet boys feel a biological imperative to go one step further. Even very smart girls are blinded into thinking that "this one is different." You know what? That one is not different.

Over the years I have known hundreds of high school "couples." I could count the people I know who married their high school sweethearts on one hand and still have fingers left over. That is because teens in our society are very rarely ready to make a lifetime commitment. Most boys feel that they are so "mature" that they have to get to first, second, third, whatever with a girl, but they're not really mature. The surest way for a girl to scare a guy off is to talk about long-term plans. Sure, there are exceptions, but in most cases the guy will admit that he's too young or "not ready" for a real commitment.

Even worse, a boy may honestly feel that he "loves" a girl, but when he gets what he's been after, his interest strangely fades. This is what the Mishna in *Avos* (5:16) means when it says that "any love that depends on something, when that thing ceases, the love will cease. But if it does not depend on anything, it will endure forever. What is an example of a love that depended on something? The love of Amnon for Tamar. What is a love that did not depend on anything? The love between David and Jonathan." We understand that David and Jonathan were the best of friends and that Jonathan, the son of King Saul, was willing to give up his chance to inherit the throne for his love of David. But who were Amnon and Tamar?

Amnon and Tamar were the children of King David, half-siblings. And Amnon was filled with lust for his half-sister, so much so that he "date raped" her. (The Nach explains how he lured her to his room under false pretenses and defiled her.) What does the Navi then tell us? "He took her, raped her and lay with her. Then Amnon despised her; the disgust he felt for her was greater than the love he had previously felt" (*II Shmuel* 13:14-15).

That pretty much sums it up. He got what he was after and he was done with her. He didn't need her any more. The Mishna tells us that this is not unique to Amnon. "*Any* love that depends on something, when that thing ceases, the love will cease."

There are other reasons why abstinence before marriage is a good idea:

- **The sexual double-standard.** Guys who sleep around are considered "players" (or, depending where you're from, "playas"). Girls are considered tramps. It's wrong, but that's the way it is.
- **You will eventually meet the right person.** Then all sorts of problems can arise. Comparing one's spouse to former lovers (especially during intimacy) can be very unhealthy for your relationship.
- **You may regret it later.** If you were shopping with your mom and met one of her former lovers from before she married your dad, would you be proud of how cool your mother was in her college days? Or would you go out to the parking lot and hide under the car until everyone was gone? Some day *you* will be the mom!
- **Premature relationships mess up other life plans.** I've seen way too many people decide where they'd go to college or whether or not to learn in Israel based in large part on accessibility to their current boyfriend or girlfriend. A year later, the boyfriend or girlfriend is usually gone, but the effects of the decision will always be there.

I could give you lots of other reasons not to get romantically involved with members of the opposite sex until engagement and marriage are viable, without even bringing religion into the discussion.

Give "sex" (at any "base" level) in hopes of receiving "love?" Not a fair trade and not a good idea.

1. Of course, we speak of "*shmiras halashon*" (watching our language) and "*mi sheshomer piv*" (one who watches his mouth), but not of being "*shomer*" the mitzvah itself.
2. Despite the fact that a handshake has more power behind it than we normally acknowledge, the intent behind a handshake in our society is a simple greeting. Accordingly, there are three schools of thought regarding a coed handshake: (a) It is a permitted gesture; (b) it is permitted to return a handshake when offered by someone who doesn't know that it is preferable not to; and (c) it is entirely prohibited, even to accept an offered hand.

   While some communities are strict, one practice in centrist Orthodox communities is to follow the moderate opinion. When a hand is extended by someone who would be offended or embarrassed should it be refused, it is, according to this opinion, considered acceptable to receive it. Of course, one should ask one's rabbi for the proper course of action in such situations, as opinions vary and this approach is far from universal.

   (Even the more lenient approach is not a blanket endorsement of all coed handshaking. If there is someone you are going to see on a regular basis, such as a co-worker, it would be advisable to teach them about your beliefs and religious practices so that you will not forever be placed in a situation requiring compromise.)
3. "*Menuval birshus haTorah*" is a colloquial term. The expression actually used in Rabbinic literature is "*naval birshus haTorah*." The Ramban coined this term in his commentary on *Vayikra* 19:2.

Selected Torah Sources pertaining to Kiruv Basar ("Negiah") and Other Sexual Issues

Negiah

> Hashem said: Do not say that since I cannot sleep with a woman that I may hold her or hug her or kiss her and it won't be a sin. Just as a nazir who may not drink wine also may not eat grapes or raisins or drink grape juice or anything that comes from a grape vine, similarly it is forbidden even to touch any woman who is not your wife. Anyone who touches a woman who is not his wife brings death upon himself (*Shemos Rabbah* 16:2).

Spiritually speaking. The main point here is that not just extramarital sex is forbidden, but any affectionate contact between the genders. If you think you've set a "safe" boundary for yourself, you're mistaken.

Promiscuity

> Do not degrade your daughter by permitting promiscuity so that the land will not become immoral and full of depravity (*Vayikra* 19:29).

While the word *l'haznosa* (to be promiscuous) has the same root as *zonah* (a prostitute), Rashi clarifies that this refers to any premarital sex.

Premarital Sex

> Blessed are you, Hashem our God, King of the universe, who sanctified us with His commandments and commanded us regarding forbidden relationships. He forbade us to be intimate with our fiancées but permitted us to be intimate with our spouses by means of chupah and kiddushin (the wedding canopy and marriage). Blessed are you, Hashem, who makes His nation holy through chupah and kiddushin (Wedding blessings)

So much for "it's okay, we're engaged!"

Extramarital Relations

> *No person may draw close to any prohibited relationship in order to initiate sexual contact (Vayikra 18:6).*

Rashi explains that even though this commandment begins with "*Ish ish*" (literally "each man"), it is given in the plural (*lo sikr'vu*, none of you may draw close) in order to include women in the prohibition.

Prostitution

> *There must not be any prostitutes among Jewish girls, nor any male prostitutes from among the sons (Devarim 23:18).*

Most commentators explain that this does not refer only to sex for money, but to any premarital sex. Rashi explains a "prostitute" in this verse to refer to a woman who makes herself available for sex.

> *Do not bring money earned from prostitution or from selling a dog for any obligation in the Beis HaMikdash because both of these are repulsive to Hashem your God (Devarim 23:19).*

One cannot do the right thing as the result of a bad deed. If someone prostitutes themselves, the money is so tainted to Hashem that He won't even let them use it for *tzedaka*.

Seduction and Rape

> *If a man seduces a virgin who is not already betrothed, he must pay a dowry and marry her (Shemos 22:15).*

> *If a man finds a virgin who is not already betrothed and rapes her, he must pay her father a dowry of 50 silver shekels. He must take the girl he raped as his wife and may not divorce her as long as he lives (Devarim 22:28-29).*

The Torah takes premarital sex very seriously. If a man forces himself on a girl, or even just talks her into it, he has to marry her. (The girl has the right to refuse; she doesn't have to marry him against her will.) If he forced himself on her, he also may not divorce her. (The reason these cases speak of a virgin who is not betrothed is because betrothal is more than engagement; it's the first step of marriage. In the case of a betrothed girl, the rapist or seducer—and the girl if she were a willing participant—would be guilty of adultery and liable to the death penalty.)

Guys are Only after One Thing

> *Rabbi Yochanan said: Man has a small organ that the more he feeds it, the hungrier it becomes, but the more he starves it, the more satisfied it becomes, as it says, "When they were starved they became satisfied" (Sukkah 52b).*

Or: it weakens him the more he feeds it, but strengthens him the more he starves it. Rashi says that constant feeding of one's lust leaves one physically depleted. Additionally, constantly gratifying his urges weakens a man's ability to withstand them.

Men Reap What They Sow

> *Rav Shmuel bar Rav Yitzchak said that when Reish Lakish would teach about the sotah (woman accused of infidelity), he would start by saying that a man is only paired with a woman according to his deeds, based upon the verse, "The scepter of the wicked shall not rest on the lot of the righteous" (Sotah 2a).*

Rashi explains this to mean that a righteous man is paired with a modest wife, while an evil man is paired with a promiscuous wife. This is a tremendous lesson for boys who want to tomcat around but still expect to marry a "nice" girl. God has no sexual "double standard."

Safeguarding a Young Lady's Dignity

> *There was a man who developed such a passion for a certain woman that it made him deathly ill. They asked the doctors who said the only thing that could save him is if she would sleep with him. The Rabbis said better he should die than she should sleep*

> with him. The doctors said to let him see her naked. The Rabbis said better he should die than see her naked. The doctors said to at least let him speak to her from behind a fence. The Rabbis said better he should die than speak to her from behind a fence (*Sanhedrin* 75a).

The Gemara then goes on to discuss why they were so strict in this situation. Even in the last case, his "cure" relied upon objectifying her. This Gemara shows the great lengths to which *Chazal* went to ensure that a young lady was not treated as an object. (You will also note that in the first case, the "only" thing that could save him was sleeping with her. By the end they were asking for a conversation from behind a fence! It's a good thing they didn't give in the first time they spoke!)

Not to Become Overly Familiar

> *A man should not inquire as to the welfare of a woman* (*Kiddushin* 70b).

Rashi explains this to mean that he should not become familiar with her, even through messengers. If he becomes too familiar, it may lead to romantic feelings.

> *Yosi ben Yochanan of Jerusalem said: your house should be open and poor people should be like members of your household and do not converse too much with the woman. This was said regarding one's own wife, even more so regarding his neighbor's wife. Based on this, the Sages said that one who speaks too much with the woman brings evil on himself, neglects the study of Torah and will ultimately inherit Gehennom (Hell)* (*Avos* 1:5).

The Mishna uses the awkward phrase "*ha'isha*" (the woman) rather than *isha* (a woman) or *nashim* (women) to specify one's own wife in the period of time each month when she is forbidden to him because it may lead to intimacy. If it's good advice regarding one's own wife, it's great advice regarding someone else's wife!

> *A man should not be overly familiar with a woman because it will inevitably lead to adultery* (*Nedarim* 20a).

A Chapter for the Boys

As previously mentioned, Judaism has dress codes for boys and for girls. Just like school dress codes, the details are not identical for both genders.

For girls, the dress code is what we typically refer to as "*tzniyus.*" But boys also have a dress code. The Torah commands males to wear *tzitzis*, placing fringes on a four-cornered garment. The Torah also commands males to wear *tefillin* every weekday, which we do during the morning prayer service. Probably the most visible part of the boys' uniform is the *yarmulke*. (This is also known as a *kippah* in Hebrew or a "skullcap" in English. Slang terms include "Yid lid.") The *yarmulke* is not a Torah requirement; it's not even Rabbinically prescribed in the strictest sense. It's a classic example of a *minhag*. While "*minhag*" means "custom," a true *minhag* is not optional. Just as the Jewish women voluntarily accepted certain standards of dress upon themselves, the head covering that men wear was voluntarily adopted by the Jewish people. Once adopted, it became required by mandate of the people. ("*Yarmulke*" comes from the Aramaic words *yara* meaning awe and *malka* meaning king. We wear the *yarmulke* to show our awe of Hashem by reminding us that He is always above us.)

This is not to say that there is not a standard of *tzniyus* for boys also. There is, but it is not the same as it is for girls. While the details may differ, the principles are the same.

Tzniyus keeps us from objectifying people, whether male or female. While a boy is permitted to bare more skin than a girl, there is still a standard of dress and comportment that is appropriate, as well as a degree that is inappropriate. The more advanced someone becomes in their Torah learning, the more sensitive they become to their manner of dress. A teenage boy, even a college student, may feel comfortable in the classroom dressed the same way they would for the football field, but the Rebbe delivering the lecture probably wouldn't.

Additionally, the boy has an obligation to facilitate the girl's *tzniyus* efforts, not to attempt to circumvent them. The Rabbis of the Talmud have some very harsh words for boys (or men) who try and "sneak a peek" at girls (or women) at moments of immodesty.

To Be Careful What We Look At

> *Avert my eyes from seeing things of no value and give me life in Your ways (Tehillim 119:37).*

There is clearly a "cause and effect" relationship between the things we choose to look at and living in the way Hashem desires. We should therefore ask His help not to be tempted to look at things that keep us from that goal.

Giving Privacy

> *Since grinding wheat does not require privacy, the owner of the property does not have to leave ... since baking does require privacy, the owner of the property must leave (Baba Kama 48a).*

Rashi explains that baking requires privacy because the woman must push her sleeves up and expose her arms. We see from this that if a woman is engaged in a practice that requires her to act or dress immodestly, men have a responsibility to give her privacy.

> *Joint owners of a courtyard may prevent one another from using it for any purpose except for washing clothes because it is not proper for Jewish girls to embarrass themselves by washing clothes in public (Baba Basra 57b).*

Rashi explains that washing clothes publicly entailed taking them to the river. The woman had to stand in the river, for which she must hike up her skirt. Even though joint owners of a property could prevent one another from using it for other purposes, it is unreasonable to expect a girl to behave in that fashion when she could wash clothes modestly in private.

Modesty Between Husband and Wife

> *There was once a man who married a woman who was missing a finger and he didn't even know it until the day she died. Rav said, "How modest was this woman that even her own husband did not recognize her!" Rabbi Chiya said to him, "That was her way, but how modest was her husband not to look at his own wife!"* (Shabbos 53b)

Rashi explains "that was her way" to mean that many women might be exceptionally modest, especially a woman such as this who was concealing a physical defect. Not to take away from the credit due to this woman, her husband was exceptionally modest for not trying to circumvent her modesty.

Scholars Have a Higher Standard

> *Rabbi Yochanan asked Rabbi Banaah how the robe of a Talmid Chacham (Torah scholar) should be. He answered that his skin should not be visible through it. He then asked how the mantle of a scholar should be. He answered that no more than a handbreadth of his robe should be visible from beneath it* (Baba Basra 57b).

While a laxer standard of dress may be acceptable for men than for women, Torah scholars are expected to adhere to a higher standard, similar to that of women. Displaying their flesh or inner garments is considered immodest for a *Talmid Chacham*. This is why you don't see pictures of *Gedolim* (Torah giants) wearing shorts and T-shirts.

Scholars Don't "Check Women Out"

> *Abaye said that a Talmid Chacham who wants to get married should take an unlearned person so that another woman is not substituted for her* (Baba Basra 168a).

Rashi clarifies that a scholar is not in the habit of examining women and might not remember her features if a switch is later made. An unlearned person is in the habit of looking at women's faces.

"Peeking" is Evil

> *Rav Chiya bar Abba says that the verse "He shuts my eyes from seeing evil" refers to one who does not look at women while they wash clothes . . . if there is another road and he does not take it, he is a rasha (wicked) (Baba Basra 57b).*

As mentioned above, washing clothes required a woman to hike up her dress and get in the river. A man who takes a path past such a sight when an alternative exists is deemed "evil." (If there is no other path, he must still avert his eyes.)

Not to Be Enticed

> *They shall be tzitzis for you so that you shall see them and remember all of God's commandments and do them and not be led after your hearts and eyes which have led you astray before (Bamidbar 15:39).*

Rashi explains that the heart and eyes are the "spies" of the body. The eyes see something, the heart desires it and the body commits sins to fulfill these desires.

Men Shouldn't Stare at Women

> *I have made a pact with my eyes. Why should I look at young girls? (Iyov 31:1)*

> *If a man stares at a woman's pinky, it is just as bad as if he stared at her genitals (Brachos 24a).*

The issue at hand is the objectification of women. If a man views a woman as a sex object, it makes no difference what part of her he is objectifying; it is always wrong.

> *A man should not walk behind a woman. Even if his wife is ahead of him on a bridge, he should move over to the side. Any man who crosses a river behind a woman will have no place in the World to Come (Brachos 61a).*

When a man walks behind a woman, what do you think he's looking at? This kind of gawking is inappropriate even if she's his wife. The reason the Gemara speaks so harshly about crossing a river after a woman is explained by Rashi. When crossing a river, a woman raises her garments and exposes herself. Since it's unavoidable for a man to stare at her, he must not cross behind her.

> *If a man counts money into a woman's hand just so he can have an excuse to look at her, even if he has Torah and good deeds comparable to those of Moshe Rabbeinu (Moses), he will not escape punishment in Gehennom (Hell), as it says, "hand to hand for evil will not go unpunished"* (Brachos 61a).

> *"You shall guard yourself from every evil thing." This verse means that one should not stare at a beautiful woman even if she is single, a married woman even if she is unattractive, or at a woman's colorful clothes . . . Rabbi Yehuda said in the name of Shmuel that this applies even if they are hanging on the wall. Rav Papa says this is only if he knows the owner* (Avodah Zara 20a-20b).

If a man stares at a garment owned by a woman he knows, it is likely that he will come to imagine her in it and fantasize about her.

> *Rabbi Acha the son of Rabbi Yoshia says that whoever gazes at women will inevitably come to sin. Whoever stares at a woman's heel will have children who act inappropriately* (Nedarim 20a).

The Gemara goes on to explain that it doesn't literally mean the heel, but is euphemistically referring to the genitals.

Appendix A

Additional Sources on Tzniyus

Assorted Laws

That Married Women Cover Their Hair

> *The kohein stands the woman (suspected of adultery) before Hashem and uncovers her hair . . . (Bamidbar 5:18).*

The *Gemara* infers from this that a married woman's hair is normally covered (*Kesubos* 72a).

Mixed Swimming

> *The trait of an evil man is not to object if his wife goes out with her hair uncovered, spins wool in public, which exposes her armpits, and bathes with men. Bathes with men! How could such a thing be possible? Rather, it means bathes in the same place as men (Gittin 90a-90b).*

The Gemara is incredulous about the possibility that men and women might go mixed swimming. It lowers the level to a case where women come and go in the sight of men, which is merely suggestive. The Sages of the Gemara would no doubt suffer fits of apoplexy if they were to see what is considered acceptable attire on beaches in the twenty-first century.

To Keep a Higher Standard

You shall be holy because I, Hashem your God, am holy (Vayikra 19:2).

Rashi says that this means to separate from sexual sins because wherever the Torah commands us to abstain from sexual immorality, it mentions holiness. He brings several examples from *Vayikra* 21 to support this assertion. We have an obligation to raise ourselves above our baser natures.

Rules that Jewish Women Accepted upon Themselves

What does "violating the law of Jewish women" mean? Going out with the head uncovered, spinning wool in public and chatting with every man. But covering the hair is a Biblical requirement! . . . Biblically, covering one's hair by carrying a basket on one's head would be permissible; according to the law of Jewish women it is unacceptable (Kesubos 72a).

Rashi explains "*das yehudis*" (the law of Jewish women) to mean extra stringencies that women collectively accepted upon themselves even though they were not originally required by the Torah. Once accepted by the community, they become binding. (An analogous male case would be the *yarmulke*, which was voluntarily accepted by the Jewish people and is as binding as any law enacted by the Rabbis.)

Davening Facing Uncovered Parts

It is forbidden to recite Shema while facing an uncovered handbreadth of a part that women normally cover—even his own wife. [Remah: This is said specifically about his own wife. In another woman, even less than a handbreadth of a part normally covered is considered private] (Orach Chaim 75:1).

A sweater with small holes throughout would be an example of an uncovered space of less than a handbreath. The commentary of the *Mishna Brurah* on this follows.

> *A part that women normally*: because this will bring a man to lustful thoughts when he looks at it. Therefore it is considered a "private" part and a man may not recite Shema or any other holy work while facing it, just as he cannot when facing actual nudity . . . **Cover**: but her hands and face, according to the practice is to allow uncovering them . . . similarly the leg up to the knee, in a place where women do not cover it one may recite Shema facing it because he is used to it and it will not give him lustful thoughts. But in a place where they cover it, the amount is a handbreadth as with other parts of a woman. Regarding the thigh and (upper) arm, even if women in that area commonly uncover them . . . it is forbidden (*Mishna Brurah* 75:1-2).

Certain things (lower leg, for example) are a matter of local custom. Other things (like the thigh) are prohibited even if "everybody's doing it."

(You will note that the law in this section pertains to the men, not to the women. As we have pointed out, *tzniyus* is not—or ought not to be—something that men just drop on women's doorstep! There are *halachos* for the guys, too!)

Tzniyus Behaviors

"Unintentional" Exposure

> *What is considered violating the law of Jewish women? . . . spinning wool in public . . . Rav Yehuda said in the name of Shmuel that this is because she exposes her arms to people* (*Kesubos* 72a).

The exposure here is unintentional; she doesn't necessarily *want* to reveal her arms. But while it may be unintentional, it is also *inevitable*. The act of spinning will invariably cause her sleeves to roll back, exposing her arms. Accordingly, to do it publicly is a violation of the laws that women voluntarily accepted upon themselves. Similarly, girls must be careful of any activities or garments that will inevitably lead to accidental exposure.

Modesty in Private

> Kimchis had seven sons, all of whom served as Kohein Gadol (High Priest) at some point. The Rabbis asked her what she did to merit this. She answered, "In my whole life, the beams of my house did not see me with my hair uncovered (*Yoma* 47a).

I listed this under "Modesty in Private" rather than under "Reward for Modesty" because the Rabbis reject Kimchis' hypothesis. The Gemara continues: Many women have done this without similar results. The fact that they don't accept her theory does not make her behavior any less praiseworthy. Compare this with the version of the Kimchis story from the *Yerushalmi* (on page 32).

Modesty in the Bathroom

> A man gave a eulogy in the presence of Rav Nachman. He said, "the deceased was modest in every way." Rav Nachman said, "how do you know? Did you ever follow him into the bathroom? Because we have learned that a person is only called modest based on the way he behaves in the bathroom (*Brachos* 62a).

> Rav Tanchum bar Chanilai said that whoever behaves modestly in the bathroom is saved from three things: from snakes, scorpions and evil spirits. Some also say that he will have pleasant dreams (*Brachos* 62a).

We see from the preceding three examples that the purpose of modesty is to hone and refine the *middos* (traits) of the woman, not to avoid lustful gazes. Even in absolute privacy, it is praiseworthy to inculcate modest habits.

What exactly is "modesty in the bathroom?" Nobody expects people to shower with their clothes on, although there are people who change clothes under a robe or a blanket, even when they are alone. Let's just say that there are certain vain, narcissistic, or even hedonistic behaviors that debase a person even when there's nobody there but the person and God. Give yourself the same respect you would hope others would grant you by acting as appropriately just for yourself as you would for others.

Removing Temptation

> *If temptation is in your hands, get rid of it. Do not let evil remain in your house* (*Iyov* 11:14).

One should not put oneself in a position where he or she may be tempted to sin. This applies equally to the stack of "fine reading material" your brother has under his mattress and to that dress that you know you shouldn't wear, but you "just look *so* good in it!"

Not Overdoing it

> *Rabbi Chanina ben Tradyon was sentenced (by the Romans) to be martyred by burning, his wife to be executed and his daughter placed in a brothel . . . why was she placed in a brothel? Rabbi Yochanan related that Rabbi Chanina's daughter was once walking past some great men of Rome who commented, "How pleasant are the footsteps of this girl!" Hearing this, she increased the precision with which she walked. This is what Rav Shimon ben Lakish meant when he quoted the verse, "the sin of my heel surrounds me." Mitzvos that we tread upon (i.e. ignore) confront us when we are judged* (*Avodah Zara* 17b-18a).

(She probably did not deserve to be placed in a brothel just for this one sin alone; more likely, it was merely a sin that "testified" against her as part of her overall package when she was judged. It was not inappropriate that her punishment was based upon some sin that was part of her package. Considering that her parents were murdered, this was probably a relatively merciful judgment.)

Appendix B

Role Models from Tanach

There is a principal in Judaism that *maaseh Avos siman l'banim*, the deeds of the fathers serve as a sign to the sons. The deeds of the founding fathers of Judaism serve as powerful lessons on honesty, morality, *chesed* (kindness) and other important character traits. Similarly, *maaseh Imahos siman l'banos*, the deeds of the mothers serve as a sign to the daughters. The founding mothers set some equally potent standards for their descendants. A handful follow.

Sarah Imeinu

> *And they said to Avraham, "where is Sarah your wife?" He responded, "She is in the tent"* (*Bereishis* 18:9).

Avraham was asked about Sarah's whereabouts by the angels who came to announce Yitzchak's birth. Rashi explains that the reason Sarah was in the tent when company came was because of her great modesty.

> *The visiting angels knew that Sarah was in the tent. So why did they ask? To make her husband appreciate her* (*Baba Metzia* 87a).

Having become used to Sarah's modest ways, Avraham might take them for granted. The angels knew where Sarah was; the purpose of asking about her whereabouts was to bring Sarah's modesty to Avraham's attention and thereby to further endear her to him.

> *As they got close to Egypt, (Avraham) said to Sarah his wife, "Now I know that you are an attractive woman" (Bereishis 12:11).*

Didn't Avraham know that his wife was attractive before this? Rashi explains that both of them were very modest. It was only because of the hardships of traveling that it was difficult for them to maintain their exceptional level of *tzniyus*. Due to the inability to maintain their usually high standards of *tzniyus*, it came to Avraham's attention just how beautiful his wife was.

Rivka Imeinu

> *And the girl (Rivka) was beautiful, a virgin, who had not had sexual relations with any man (Bereishis 24:16).*

If she was a virgin, wouldn't we know that she hadn't had sexual relations with any man? Rashi explains that the girls where Rivka grew up protected their virginity but did "everything but." The extra words explain that Rivka did not engage in these practices, either.

> *Rivka looked up and saw Yitzchak, so she got down from the camel. She asked the servant, "who is that man coming from the field to greet us?" The servant answered her, "that is my master," so she covered herself with her veil (Bereishis 24:64-65).*

Rivka's modesty is evident from the fact that she covered herself with a veil, but why did I include the previous verse about getting down from the camel? The commentators give a number of explanations for this, many of which revolve around Rivka's great modesty. The Rashbam explains that, as one can't really ride a camel side-saddle, Rivka had to ride like a man, straddling the camel. When she arrived and saw Yitzchak, she quickly jumped down from her immodest position.

Rachel and Leah

> *Eisav looked up and saw the women and children. He asked Yaakov, "who are they to you?" (Yaakov) answered, "these are the children that Hashem has been kind enough to give me" (Bereishis 33:5).*

If Eisav asked about the women and children, why did Yaakov only answer him about the children? The Ramban explains that it was because of the modesty of Rachel and Leah. Just as Sarah stayed in the tent while Avraham entertained male visitors, Rachel and Leah also did not mingle with men.

Esther

> *When Esther's turn arrived . . . to be brought to the king, she did not request anything except that which Hegai told her . . . and Esther found favor in the eyes of all who saw her* (Esther 2:15).

Esther shunned all the cosmetics and finery which were offered to beautify her for her appearance before the king. She relied on her own natural beauty and was found to be the most pleasing of all the girls. This was no doubt *because* she favored her own beauty over being artificially "enhanced," not *despite* it.

Ruth

> *Boaz said to the young man in charge of the harvesters, "whose young woman is that?"* (Ruth 2:5)

Rashi asks why Boaz asked about Ruth. He answers that Boaz was curious about Ruth's great modesty. She would glean upright stalks standing and stalks on the ground while sitting, rather than stretching or bending. This way her sleeve would not roll back (when reaching up) and her hemline would not ride up (when bending down). While this may have been meant to avoid the advances of the coarser farmhands, it attracted the attention of the more refined Boaz, who was the spiritual leader of the generation. (Being great or holy does not make people incapable of being attracted to the opposite gender, it just makes them more likely to be attracted to the person's positive qualities, rather than to their physicality.)

Devorah

> *Devorah, the wife of Lapidos, was a prophetess. She judged Israel at that time. She sat beneath Deborah's Palm Tree, between Ramah*

and Beis-El in the hills of Ephraim. All Israel came to her for judgment (Shoftim 4:4-5).

She met people outside so as to avoid a problem with *yichud*, the prohibition of men and women being secluded together. While *yichud* could have been avoided simply by leaving the door open, Devorah's high position and natural modesty compelled her to take additional measures upon herself.

Appendix C

Immodesty

While we always try to accentuate the positive, we must also recognize the consequences of the negative. The Torah has much to say in praise of modesty, but it likewise has a few harsh words for the alternative.

Chastised for Immodesty

> *From the sole of the foot up to the head, no part is unblemished (Yeshaya 1:6).*

The prophet Yeshaya criticized the people of Israel for their sins, including their immodesty and inappropriate behavior, to which the choice of words in this verse alludes. (Contrast this with the praise of *Shir HaShirim* 4:7, "All of you is beautiful, my love, there is no fault in you.")

Sin of Immodesty

> *God says: Because the girls of Israel have become full of themselves, walking with stretched necks and heavily made-up eyes, walking with deliberate steps and tinkling feet, therefore God will bare the heads of the daughters of Israel and God will reveal their nakedness. On that day God will remove the glory of their anklets and tiaras, necklaces and earrings, bracelets, scarves, hats, armbands, belts, perfume and amulets, rings and nose rings, cloaks, wraps, gowns,*

> *handbags, wispy dresses and linen robes, handkerchiefs and veils (Yeshaya 3:16-23).*

There's a lot said in these verses. Let's take it in several stages:

First of all, notice that the immodesty follows the sense of pride and haughtiness that the girls of Israel felt. It was their egos that made the girls think it was necessary to dress and act in this way.

There are several explanations about what it means to walk with an outstretched neck. The tall girls wanted to make themselves appear even more statuesque and attract greater attention to themselves. They would walk between two shorter girls to appear taller or wear shoes with exceptionally high heels. Alternatively, they wore outrageously inflated hair styles.

They walked with deliberate steps, calculated to attract attention. Any girl reading this surely knows that it is possible to perform an act as basic as walking in a seductive fashion. (Contrast this with *Micha* 6:8, "He told you what is good and what Hashem desires of you . . . to walk modestly with God" and with *Shir HaShirim* 7:2, "How beautiful are your footsteps in your shoes, Princess.")

The *Navi* (prophet) also criticizes the excessive and immodest use of make-up and perfume. (See *Shabbos* 62b for the explanation of this section of *Sefer Yeshaya*.)

Rashi explains that they wore veils to hide their faces, not out of modesty but to create a sense of mystery. Guys would become curious for a peek and would be enticed by the fleeting glimpses they would receive.

The garments listed in these verses include such seemingly innocuous garments as belts. The *Gemara* (*Sotah* 8b) explains that even belts can be used to attract men.

Consequences of Immodest Behavior

> *Leah's daughter Dina, whom she bore to Yaakov, went out to meet the local girls. She was seen by Shechem, the son of Chamor the*

> *Chivite, who was ruler of that land. (Shechem) took her, raped her and sodomized her (Bereishis* 34:1-2).

The Midrash (*Bereishis Rabbah* 80 and *Etz Yosef* there) explains that Dina went out immodestly, with her arms and face uncovered, contrary to the accepted practice in her area. This aroused Shechem who then raped her.

Similar to this is the case of Shlomis bas Divri (see *Vayikra* 24:11). This is presumably a pseudonym. Rashi explains that she was called *Shlomis* from the word "Shalom," the standard form of greeting in Hebrew. She felt compelled to go and greet everyone she saw. *Bas Divri*, the daughter of words, because she was overly chatty. Her boisterous nature attracted the attention of an Egyptian taskmaster who raped her and fathered a child who grew up to curse Hashem. Even though she was raped, Rashi uses the harsh term *zonah* (slut) when discussing her because her behavior was so clearly inappropriate.

It is important to clarify that, while inappropriate dress and behavior can inspire others to inappropriate acts, **those other people are not excused for their actions**. Both Shechem and the Egyptian were harshly punished. The Torah says in no uncertain terms that rape is like murder and **the victim is blameless** (*Devarim* 22:26). Nevertheless, we must still exercise good judgment.

(A non-*tzniyus* analogy: Don't walk through bad neighborhoods flashing your money. If you get mugged, you're innocent and the thief is guilty, but you still showed poor judgment.)

What They're Saying About The Nach Yomi Companion

"*The Nach Yomi Companion* is an invaluable resource for novices and scholars alike. It integrates multiple sources to give the reader a thorough understanding not just of the text of a specific chapter, but also how that chapter fits into the larger Biblical picture. This book belongs on every well-stocked Jewish bookshelf."
—*Aliza Libman Baronofsky, Tanach teacher and dean of students, Maimonides School, Brookline, MA*

"*(The Nach Yomi Companion)* is one of the best-kept secrets… It is a one-of-a-kind book that I've been wanting for years. Not everybody is able to do an in-depth study of Nach. This gives a brief chapter-by-chapter summary in a very readable format."
—*Rabbi Tzali Freedman, Regional Director, Central East NCSY*

"Rabbi Jack Abramowitz… knows when to be brief (i.e., skip) and when to give details. … However, the key to his success is in his keen sense of what speaks to people today. His writing is filled with puns and pop-culture references, but also with lessons that are very relevant to our daily lives. What emerges is not just a summary of the Bible or a commentary on it. It is an application of the Bible to today's world, a lesson in the eternal value of the Bible. If you are interested in learning quickly what the Bible is all about, then this is the book for you. Call it the Cliff Notes to the Jewish Bible."
—*Rabbi Gil Student, Hirhurim - Musings*

CPSIA information can be obtained
at www.ICGtesting.com
Printed in the USA
BVOW08s2133151216
470971BV00001B/22/P

9 781441 577962